BRIGHT NOTES

THE SECOND SEX BY SIMONE DE BEAUVOIR

Intelligent Education

Nashville, Tennessee

BRIGHT NOTES: The Second Sex
www.BrightNotes.com

No part of this publication may be used or reproduced in any manner whatsoever without written permission, except in the case of brief quotations in critical articles and reviews. For permissions, contact Influence Publishers http://www.influencepublishers.com.

ISBN: 978-1-645423-92-8 (Paperback)
ISBN: 978-1-645423-93-5 (eBook)

Published in accordance with the U.S. Copyright Office Orphan Works and Mass Digitization report of the register of copyrights, June 2015.

Originally published by Monarch Press.
James R. Lindroth, Colette Lindroth, 1988
2019 Edition published by Influence Publishers.

Interior design by Lapiz Digital Services. Cover Design by Thinkpen Designs.

Printed in the United States of America.

Library of Congress Cataloging-in-Publication Data forthcoming.
Names: Intelligent Education
Title: BRIGHT NOTES: The Second Sex
Subject: STU004000 STUDY AIDS / Book Notes

CONTENTS

1)	Introduction To Simone De Beauvoir	1
2)	Themes	22
3)	Structure, Style, Syntax	25
4)	Textual Analysis	
	Book One: Facts And Myths	37
	Book Two: Woman's Life Today	65
5)	Critics Respond To The Second Sex	103
6)	Ideas For Papers, Oral Reports, And Class Discussion	115
7)	Bibliography	120

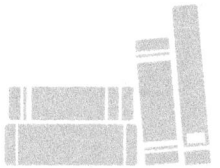

INTRODUCTION TO SIMONE DE BEAUVOIR

BY WALTER JAMES MILLER, EDITOR, MONARCH NOTES, PROFESSOR OF ENGLISH, NEW YORK UNIVERSITY

When - according to Simone de Beauvoir - did woman become inferior to man? Why is woman an easy prey to male domination? Why have women never rebelled against their male oppressors, as the Irish and the blacks have challenged theirs? Why has there never been a female Shakespeare or a female Beethoven? Why does de Beauvoir call marriage? "woman's biggest trap"?

In what ways is *The Second Sex* based on de Beauvoir's own life-style? How does her literary style resemble that of the Bible?

These and many other equally interesting questions are taken up in this Monarch Note. But it will have little meaning for you unless you have already read or are now reading *The Second Sex* (Vintage Books: Random House). The author, editors, and publishers of this study-guide assume it will prompt you often to refer to your copy of de Beauvoir's masterpiece.

BRIGHT NOTES STUDY GUIDE

THE SECOND SEX: ITS PLACE IN HISTORY

Few books have contributed to the expansion of human consciousness as has *The Second Sex* by the French writer and philosopher Simone de Beauvoir. If Freud's *The Interpretation of Dreams* (1900) opened the twentieth century to psychology - the understanding of man's inner world and the power of his sexuality - de Beauvoir's *The Second Sex* (1949) opened the second half of the twentieth century to the reevaluation of women's role throughout history in a world dominated by men, and subsequently, to women's continuing struggle for emancipation and equality.

The Second Sex, published in France in two volumes, was an immediate success. Its first volume appeared in June 1949 and sold 22,000 copies in one week; the second appeared the following November and sold as well. Even before publication, three chapters had appeared in issues of *Les Temps Modernes*, and each issue was snatched from the newsstands. In 1953 it appeared in English translation and sold two million copies. It was translated into fifteen languages, and stayed on the bestseller list for a year in Japan.

Immediately it unleashed an unparalleled storm of controversy, evoking both praise and outrage. Simone de Beauvoir herself became the subject of admiration as well as of insult and mockery.

The Second Sex was much ahead of its time. It had been only four years prior to its appearance that women in France had finally won the right to vote. (In the USA women had won this right in 1920, with the passage of the Nineteenth Amendment to the Constitution.) As a matter of fact, a regressive period for women was already long under way by 1949, the year of the book's publication. This was the period immediately following World War II, when men were returning from the front to reclaim those jobs that had been filled by women. Dutifully, most women returned to their homes amidst a general euphoria accompanied by a cultural blitz that hailed the "true woman" as synonymous with wife, homemaker, and mother. The baby-boom followed.

INFLUENCE IN USA

Fourteen years passed after the publication of *The Second Sex* before the women's movement emerged. That much time was needed for Simone de Beauvoir's radical ideas to ferment and for women to absorb them. In 1963 *The Feminine Mystique* by the American feminist Betty Friedan appeared and became a best-seller, having a tremendous influence as a consciousness-raiser among American women. Although in her book Better Friedan did not acknowledge her debt to Simone de Beauvoir, years later she admitted that it was de Beauvoir who had started here on the new road. Friedan adapted de Beauvoir's ideas and simplified them to make them accessible to American women. She offered women the vision of equality within the system, while de Beauvoir insisted that only a restructuring of society would enable women to gain true equality. If Simone de Beauvoir was, and still is, the theoretician of the women's liberation movement, Betty Friedan rendered the theory more tangible and made de Beauvoir's ideas less revolutionary, more practical and accessible. In 1966, two years after the publication of *The Feminine Mystique*. NOW (The National Organization for Women) was founded in the USA. Three years after the formation of NOW the women's movement began to organize in France but didn't come into the forefront until 1971.

THE BIBLE FOR FEMINISTS

The Second Sex serves as the stepping stone for all other feminists' work. The eruption of the women's liberation movement years after the appearance of her radical study of womankind places Simone de Beauvoir as the uncontested mother figure of the movement. Although many feminists continue to take issue with some of her ideas, and others question her radical solution, they all acknowledge her, and in the process have produced many new studies and scholarly papers. These studies have encouraged scholars to investigate areas of womankind never probed before, and have turned women's studies into a serious academic discipline in many universities. Simone de Beauvoir became a cult figure for many, and *The Second Sex* became required reading, a sort of Bible, for feminists. In spite of many serious reservations, it is still valid and powerful as a consciousness-raiser and as a classic in the field.

The Second Sex does not deal only with women's condition and need for independence. In fact, it calls for a sweeping and radical revamping of an entire society. If women, half of the world population, will change their lives and become, like men, economically and emotionally independent, men too will be forced to change their lives. Not only will an equal number of women and men be in the workforce, but women also will compete with men. With women out of the home, the responsibilities of organizing the family and caring for children will have to be shared. Signs of this change are already visible in many places.

The year 1974, the 25th anniversary of *The Second Sex*, saw numerous conferences, essays, and a general celebration that epitomized *The Second Sex* as the classic study of woman. On its 30th anniversary in September 1979, a three-day conference. "*The Second Sex* - Thirty Years Later" was held at New York University and attended by over 800 women (and a few men) who came from throughout the United States and from abroad. At the conference, which featured presentations on women, culture, and society, it was acknowledged that *The Second Sex* still remains the only thorough attempt to understand the situation of modern women from a historical, economic, sociological, psychological, and literary point of view. The conference acknowledged the immense excitement that the book still generates among current feminists, and the debt they owe de Beauvoir.

The French minister at the recently founded Ministry of Women's Rights, Yvette Roudy, has summed up the importance of de Beauvoir's achievement in *Because of Them* (1985)

> **If there had not been Simone de Beauvoir's very complete, very solid, and enduringly true theoretical and historical analysis, the effects of the women's movement struggles which sprang up around 1968 would not have been as powerful.**
>
> **I do not think that any movement, whatever it might be, can thrive unless it is based on a serious, coherent analysis of the situation, and it is the framework furnished by Simone de Beauvoir that permits us to work and advance even today. If I had not read *The Second Sex* and other texts by Simone de Beauvoir, I would not have the self-assurance which I do to continue the task I'm in the process of accomplishing.**

SIMONE DE BEAUVOIR: A WOMAN WHO LIVED LIKE A MAN

Simone de Beauvoir's life is as revolutionary as her book *The Second Sex*. In her life, she put into practice the ideas she advocated in her famous book: a woman should be economically and emotionally independent and live to her full potential as a human being. Although today we see more and more such independent women, it was almost unheard of when Simone de Beauvoir was growing up in the beginning of this century. She actually had the courage and the strength of conviction to live like a man. Many women looked up to her with admiration and sought to imitate her way of living. No wonder that she became a model and symbol for the new woman.

At a time when women's main function in life was conceived as being housewives, wives, and mothers, Simone de Beauvoir rejected home, marriage, and motherhood. Refusing to be enslaved to a house, she lived in hotels. Refusing to be dependent on a man or to serve one, she rejected marriage and worked for her living. To fulfill her potential as a human being, she dedicated her life to her writing career. She had a lifelong relationship with a man without marrying him or even living with him - a moral sin and inconceivable behavior in the thirties, especially for a woman. To exercise complete freedom and experience the richness of life, she took lovers and kept her relationships in the open.

In short, she took complete charge of her life, inventing the kind of life she wanted to live. *The Second Sex* is a call for women to take charge of their lives, to choose freedom and independence rather than servitude to men.

De Beauvoir herself was rigidly educated to yield to authority, be it parental or religious, and to conform to the decorum and constraint of her upper social class. The fact that she rebelled and rejected her social and religious background gives credit to her very inquisitive and intelligent mind that questioned received ideas and every **convention**, while constructing an altogether different life for herself.

"I have never met anyone in the whole of my life who was so well equipped for happiness as I was, or who labored so stubbornly to achieve it," she wrote in the second volume of her autobiography. That happiness is not a matter of mere luck but of choice and hard work; that people are responsible for the kind of lives they live; and that being happy is a matter of personal decision - these are profound and daring concepts. They definitely worked in Simone de Beauvoir's case.

THE EARLY YEARS

Simone de Beauvoir was born on January 9, 1908 in Paris, a city she loved and where she lived all her life. The family had an apartment overlooking the Boulevard Raspail in Montparnasse, the "Greenwich Village" of Paris. Simone and her younger sister, Helene, used to watch passers - by from their balcony, with Simone inventing lives for them.

Home was besieged by contradictions. Although both her parents came from the upper class, they could not afford living in accordance with their class, and the gap between their social standing and their economic standard created a keen and perennial tension that cast its shadow over all their lives. Her father, George, a handsome, life-loving man, was a lawyer by profession, though he hardly practiced it, and an actor by passion. He loved the theatre but his social status prevented him from pursuing a career in the theatre. Still, he spent much of his free time acting with amateur groups and associating with theatre people who often filled the house with merriment and recitation.

"Bourgeois marriage ... unnatural"

Her father's joy of life and devout individualism contrasted greatly with her mother's rigid conventionalism. Simone's mother came from a richly bourgeois, Catholic family. She was promised a large dowry when she married George de Beauvoir, but her father, a banker, was forced into bankruptcy - a disgrace and a crime at the time - when Simone was one year old. From that time her mother continuously felt guilty and responsible for the family's near-poverty situation. She took upon herself the role of caring for the household without any servants, but became very bitter as a result. "Outdated ideas prevented her from working away from home," wrote Simone years later; had she done it "she would have risen in her own esteem . . .she would have escaped from a state of dependence that tradition made her think natural but that did not . . .agree with her nature." Her mother was very formal and rigid, "her heart and mind had been squeezed into an armor of principles and prohibitions," and from an early age Simone knew that she was not going to live like her mother. And when she observed her father coming home in the early hours of the morning after having visited one of his women friends, smelling of liquor - and her mother's silent bitterness - she concluded that "bourgeois marriage is an unnatural institution."

Simone was "a madly gay little girl," brimming with energy and "very, very happy" although from an early age she was prone to fits of rage, falling to the ground in convulsions, her face turning purple. She was very gifted and learned to read at three, reciting poems and little stories her father had taught her, or which she wrote herself. At seven her proud parents bound her stories into a book. The evenings would pass with her father reading aloud to his family from the great classics, and often they would act and recite together. Simone grew up to love books and learning and to think that to be an author was the greatest occupation.

But the family was relatively poor, and long into her teens Simone and her sister wore their rich cousins' hand-me-down dresses. Her parents were too poor to have her educated at home by governesses as were her cousins and the other children of the upper class. At the age of five she attended a very rigid religious school, but she loved learning and rose to the top of her class. There she met her classmate Zaza, a vivacious, bright little girl, and the two became inseparable for years.

A REBEL AT 12

When she was 12 Simone began to rebel against her parents and question the validity of their values. This soon led her to lose faith in religion and to reject bourgeois **conventions** and modes of behavior. Following a heated argument, she would often hear her father say, "Simone has a man's brain; she thinks like a man; she is a man."

Financially the situation at home deteriorated and the family had to move to a smaller and less expensive apartment. Knowing that there would be no dowries for the girls and therefore no possibility of marriage, her father encouraged his daughters to study. "My dears," he told them, bitterly acknowledging his failure, "you'll have to work for your living." But later, when Simone did just what he had told her, he resented her for it and she was very hurt. She expressed the turbulence of her feeling in the diary she had been keeping. At 15, when she was asked what she would be later in life, she answered, "a famous author," and she obsessively pursued the goal she had set for herself.

Excelling In Studies

Simone decided to continue her studies in the university, although it was unheard of for a girl of her class. She excelled in all her studies, which consisted of literature, mathematics, Latin, and philosophy, but even her amassing of diplomas did not satisfy her father, who rejected a daughter with the brain of a man. She was often lonely and depressed, and in her diary at that time of her life, words such as "solitude," "exile," and "rejection" repeatedly appear.

When she was 19 she received her diploma in general philosophy and ranked second in her class. "I was now on my way to the future," she wrote. Although her upbringing had convinced her of her "sex's intellectual inferiority, a fact admitted by many women," she felt triumphant when she had passed the selective examination the first time after having been told that a woman could not pass it before the fifth or sixth time: "I certainly didn't regret being a woman; on the contrary it afforded me great satisfaction.

In 1929, three unforgettable events took place. First, her closest friend, Zaza, tragically died at the age of 21 of brain fever. Her illness was apparently the result of a broken heart followed by a deep depression after her Catholic parents had prevented her from marrying the man she loved. For many years Simone believed that she had paid for "my own freedom with her death."

Second, Simone, at 21, was finally allowed to leave home and rent a room in her grandmother's house. At long last she was independent, earning her living by teaching philosophy: she was the first woman to teach in a boys' lycee.

Third, she met her lifelong companion. While she was "furiously" studying for the most prestigious and competitive agregation examination in philosophy at the Sorbonne, she met Jean-Paul Sartre, who would prove to be the most distinguished philosopher and thinker of the twentieth century. He too was studying for the same difficult examination. That same year both Sartre and de Beauvoir passed the agregation in philosophy: he ranked first, she second. Life seemed to open up for them.

SIMONE DE BEAUVOIR AND JEAN-PAUL SARTRE

Thus began a most unusual and creative relationship, a unique love story and a model for many young people who sought to imitate them. Theirs was a true marriage of minds, a profound mutual understanding. Sartre was "the double in whom I found all my burning aspiration," she later wrote in her autobiography. All her "most remote and deep-felt longings were now fulfilled." He was her "dream-companion" who would never go out of her life. Together they decided on the kind of relationship they would have: they would not marry, would not live together, would always come first for each other, yet they would be free to experience other relationships, which would be "contingent" to their "essential" one, as Sartre termed it. At his suggestion they agreed to be completely open and honest with each other.

Sartre was already known for his passion for women, but that Simone endorsed the agreement was extremely courageous for a woman at that time. In the second volume of her autobiography, she wrote what years later would antagonize many of her feminist admirers: "My trust in him was so complete that he supplied me with the sort of absolute unfailing security that I had once had from my parents, or from God." It was Sartre who set the tone of their relationship, and one wonders what kind of relationship these two would have had if it had been she who had set the tone. After all, she did experience emotional pain when Sartre became passionately attached to other women, and she was anxious to hear that she came first in his mind. In her relationship with other men, she became more conventional and even lived with one for six years. But both Sartre and de Beauvoir stubbornly kept their agreement, even when the other people involved showed less understanding or were less able to adjust.

NO COMPROMISE

Having passed the examination, Simone was assigned to teach in Marseille and Sartre in Le Havre - 500 miles apart. He offered her marriage so that they could have a joint assignment. She refused to compromise her principles of individual freedom, and she left alone for Marseille.

Once there she began her habit of very long solitary hikes - something she would continue into old age - but hiking alone on the mountains was unbefitting a lady, and people were gossiping. Later she would go camping with friends, and when people learned that a lady had spent the night with men in the same tent they were outraged. She did not mind and went on hiking and camping, dressing extravagantly, defying all conventions. She horrified adults and fascinated her students; she was adventurous and daring. For her, "happiness was absolutely everywhere," and she was determined "to look for it, to find it, and to keep it."

DE BEAUVOIR THE WRITER

The following year, in 1932, she managed to be transferred to Rouen, an hour's train ride from Paris. She was busily working on her fifth novel; the first four she had rejected as not being good enough. In Rouen she developed a close relationship with one of her students, Olga, with whom Sartre would soon have a passionate affair. With amazing honesty and openness, de Beauvoir wrote in her diary about this difficult time, "Little by little I began to compromise: my need to agree with Sartre on all subjects outweighed the desire to see Olga through eyes other than his." Unable to detach herself from the triangle, Simone became exhausted and contracted pneumonia. The story of this "dazzling trio" found its literary expression in de Beauvoir's first published novel, *She Came to Stay*, which would be published ten years later with immediate success.

Finally, in 1936, de Beauvoir was appointed to teach in a lycee in Paris. She and Sartre were now deeply involved in a circle of close friends, among whom were some of the most brilliant minds of the era, including Maurice Merlau-Ponty, Raymond Aron, and Paul Nizan. She made a habit of writing for hours in cafes. These became the center of her very active social life, which included holding discussions and socializing with friends long into the night.

DE BEAUVOIR THE NOVELIST AND ESSAYIST

In September 1939 World War II broke out and Sartre was mobilized. In 1940 the Nazis entered Paris, and France capitulated. Sartre was taken a prisoner of war, and de Beauvoir tried to sneak into the camp to visit him. He was released, unharmed, a year later. During the war years de Beauvoir used to take long bicycle rides to the country in search of food, and for the first time in her life found herself doing what she hated, cooking. She continued writing in her habitual cafe, since the only heated places in Paris were the public ones. In 1943, during the occupation, *She Came to Stay* established her reputation as a writer. A year later she published a 123-page essay, *Pyrrhus and Cineas*, written in three months. In this essay she stated her main philosophy of life, which she would later elaborate in *The Second Sex*: "We must take control of our life; because of the mere fact that we exist, we must resist temptation to be lazy and indifferent and take actions to give meaning to our life."

The war years were a turning point in de Beauvoir's life. From being wholly dedicated to literature and writing, she, together, with Sartre, came to be a dedicated political activist. The war and the Nazi occupation made her realize for the first time that she was not in total charge of her life, that external forces beyond her control had bearing on her life, too. She could not control every turn of event and at last had to admit that her life was not "a story of my own telling, but a compromise between myself and the world at large." With her usual intensity and passion, she plunged into her new faith - believing in the power of politics to create a better world. As early as the last years of the war, Sartre and de Beauvoir had organized a small resistance group of intellectuals and engaged in publishing clandestine material. Her memoirs of the period following the war are replete with the woes of the world and a detailed account of her activities concerning Algeria, Korea, China, USSR, Vietnam, and Cuba as well as her participation in the student demonstrations in Paris in May 1968.

DE BEAUVOIR THE PLAYWRIGHT

Immediately after the war and the liberation of Paris, both Sartre and de Beauvoir enjoyed instant literary success and fame. In 1945 she published her novel *The Blood of Others*, and her play *Who Shall Die?* was performed. The play presents a very intriguing philosophical question: a 14th-century town under siege is facing a difficult dilemma; if food is equally rationed, supplies will run out and all will starve, but if only the soldiers are fed and the "useless months" - women, children, the ill, and the aged - are left to starve, the town will be able to stand the siege much longer. The protagonist convinces the town to let everyone decide his own destiny.

At this time, Sartre published his famous works *Being and Nothingness* (1943) and *The Age of Reason* (1945) in which he explained his philosophy, later named existentialism. At the same time Sartre, de Beauvoir, and other political activists began to publish the influential existentialist and politically involved journal *Les Temps Modernes*. Right after the war people were hungry for culture and literature and every piece of writing was greeted with much acclaim. Sartre and de Beauvoir became celebrities, and each piece of their writing, or revelation of their lives, attracted attention and publicity.

EXISTENTIALISM

Developed in France during World War II, existentialism offered man a way to deal with the severe hardship and despair of the war and its aftermath. It shifted the focus from society, religion, and government to the individual, handling him the control over his own life.

Existentialism, based on the supremacy of man's consciousness and his awareness of self, centers around two fundamental concepts: freedom and choice. Man, who is a conscious being, has the freedom of action that enables him to overcome his problems, although external forces can impose limits on his freedom. Man realizes his existence by making free choices, and he is fully responsible for them.

Existentialism fired the popular imagination and Sartre became one of the most admired personalities of the post-war era. For the first time, philosophy descended from its lofty academic domain into the street to meet the needs of ordinary people by offering them a way out of the traumas of the war.

Although de Beauvoir helped Sartre to formulate his ideas, closely edited all his writing, and used his theories to explain her own ideas, she always openly claimed that Sartre, not she, is the philosopher; she is the writer.

THE SECOND SEX

Early in 1946, de Beauvoir felt that she wanted to write directly about herself. Sartre suggested that she should examine the way being a woman had influenced her life. De Beauvoir answered that as a woman she had never felt inferior and that being a woman did not hinder her in any way. But Sartre repeated his suggestion. "All the same, you weren't brought up in the same way as a boy would have been; you should look into it further." She did. She threw herself into the work of finding an answer to this seemingly simple question: What Is A Woman? The result is the prodigious book *The Second Sex*. In two-and-a-half years - a relatively short time for such a dense two-volume book - she researched the subject and wrote more than 1,000 pages.

De Beauvoir applied the existentialist philosophy to her analysis of the condition of woman, and proved herself to be a masterful interpreter of the psychology of woman. Instead of defending the individual against social and religious systems as the existentialists did, she made woman the center of her study, defending her against society in general and man in particular.

In 1947, while still working on *The Second Sex*, de Beauvoir undertook a university lecture tour throughout the United States, which she later described in *America Day by Day*. The American public was fascinated by her elegance, beauty, and energy, and she was fascinated by the "American dynamism" and the "magnificent triumph of man." In Chicago she met the American writer Nelson Algren (author of the now classic *The Man with the Golden Arm*), and they fell deeply in love with each other. This intense relationship lasted six years and included several trips across the Atlantic, but finally ended painfully for both, as Algren found that a relationship with a woman who lived across the ocean - and who kept first commitment to another man - was unbearable.

In June 1949 *The Second Sex* was published and Simone de Beauvoir's name burst upon the international scene. The book provoked an avalanche of indignation and rage. The noted writer Francois Mauriac began a violent crusade replete with indecent diatribe against the book and its writer. However, this only helped call attention to the book and spread de Beauvoir's words.

WOMEN AS SECOND-CLASS CITIZENS

The scandal was inevitable. The groundbreaking book exploded the confines of what both women and men understood to be woman's role in society and demolished the premise that woman is intrinsically inferior and subservient to man. The book shook established notions and centuries-old traditions, questioning what for ages people had taken for granted. Women, she claimed, constitute half of the world population yet they are only second-class citizens in a world controlled by men; women are the "inessential," dominated by men who are the "essential." While men are independent and have lives of their own, women live only in relation to men. Consequently, they are dependent and passive, not in charge of their own lives, spending their energy and abilities enslaved to others. The only way for women to become fulfilled human beings is to have a job outside the house, be economically independent like men, and stay away from marriage and motherhood.

These were revolutionary ideas. A work of this stature requires the ability to question what others take for granted, putting under a microscope "truths" and customs accepted for generations. And de Beauvoir turned upside down established notions and modes of behavior that others saw as natural. She called into question laws, customs, religions, and traditions underlying the very relationship between man and woman, offering us a different way of looking at society and at ourselves.

AFTER THE SECOND SEX

Fame opened many opportunities and the possibility to travel - and de Beauvoir loved traveling. Together with Sartre or by herself she traveled to Spain, Mexico (with Algren), Africa, and later to China, the Soviet Union, Cuba, and the Middle East.

In 1952, when she was 44, she began a long relationship with Claude Lanzmann, a young man seventeen years her junior, the kind of adventure generally reserved for men. For the first time she agreed to live with a man. They lived together for six years, but this arrangement did not prevent her from spending her summers with Sartre in Rome.

In 1954 she published *The Mandarins*, possibly her most famous novel, in which she told, in fictional form, of her relationship with Algren. The novel, dedicated to him, won the prestigious Prix Goncourt. Algren, far from being proud or grateful, was furious that she had made the details of their relationship public domain. But for de Beauvoir, as for many writers, life was but raw material for her books, and through the understanding of herself she sought to understand the world. That was the primary reason she decided to write and publish her memoirs, in which she recorded every detail and nuance of her life and of the life of family, friends, lovers, and everyone with whom she had come in contact (although she did use pseudonyms for some of the people, a thin disguise for those constantly in the public eye).

Her openness provoked strong reaction and controversy. According to Algren she was "the most hated and the most loved woman in France." According to the literary critic Henri Peyre, she has, since the end of World War II, "towered above all other women writers in her own country and probably in continental Europe."

When her mother died of cancer in 1963, she recorded the process of dying with clinical precision. Writing of her dying mother allowed her to renew "the dialogue that had been broken off during my adolescence and that our differences and our likenesses had never allowed us to take up again. And the early tenderness that I had thought dead forever came to life again." *A Very Easy Death*, a short and intense book, is considered by many to be one of her best.

DISINTEGRATION OF A MIND

After Sartre died in April 1980, de Beauvoir wrote, *Adieu: A Farewell to Sartre*, a detailed description of the daily progression of age, illness, the decline of a genius, and the "scandal of death." Some readers were incensed by the book and thought it was sacrilege to expose the decline and deterioration of a genius, the disintegration of such a mind, but de Beauvoir was, as always, in search of the truth: Sartre was human, not a monument.

From an early age de Beauvoir had been terrified by death. In 1970 she made use of this obsession in her long and intensely researched book, *The Coming of Age*. Now, reaching her sixties, she was ready to deal with aging and its consequences. If in *The Second Sex* she fought for the liberation of women, in *The Coming of Age* she fought for the liberation of the elderly from the constraints and prejudices of society. In it she meticulously analyzes the painful reality, asking questions about aging, without offering answers. The book, another consciousness-raiser, provoked wide discussions in France and abroad.

SOCIALISTS AND FEMINISTS

Until about 1970, the time of the emergence of the women's movement in France, de Beauvoir, surprisingly, was not an active feminist, even though she continued to discuss the oppression of women in interviews, essays, and introductions. She believed that her active role on behalf of socialism and human rights would naturally include strengthening women's rights. When she realized, however, that even devout socialists and human rights activists accepted as natural women's secondary role in society, she became an active feminist and gladly lent her name and fame for "political provocation." When in October 1970 she was asked to sign a manifesto in support of legalized abortion, she signed, along with other famous women, acknowledging that she, too, had had an abortion. Moreover, she allowed her studio to be used for performing abortions. The story was widely reported in many countries. In June 1972 she became the president of the Choisir Association, which included well-known people active in making free contraception available, legalizing abortions, and assuming the cost of defending women who had undergone illegal abortions. However, de Beauvoir never joined any party or organization and was always true to her decision to work outside them, a stand that made her both the most esteemed and the most hated of feminists.

In the last years of her life she wrote little but continued to be politically active. Although she lived alone, she developed a close relationship with a young woman, Sylvie Lebon, whom she later adopted. Simone de Beauvoir died on April 14, 1986, one day before the sixth anniversary of Sartre's death. They were buried on the same day, April 19, and share the same grave.

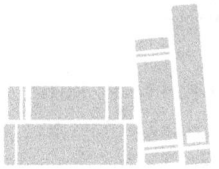

THE SECOND SEX

THEMES

1. Throughout history women have always been subordinate to men. "Woman has always been man's dependent, if not his slave; the two sexes have never shared the world in equality." In work and in motherhood, woman is more of a servant than an associate. "This has always been a man's world."

2. While man can think of himself without woman, she cannot think of herself without man. While he is the essential, the Subject, she is the incidental, the inessential, the Object, the Other.

3. Neither woman's biological nor psychological makeup is responsible for the inferior condition of woman. It is society that has made woman subordinate to man. "One is not born, but rather becomes, a woman."

4. In the age of the club and the wild beast, man's superior muscular strength was a decisive advantage to compare with woman's physical weakness, which constituted "a glaring inferiority." But the invention of the machine has

made woman's physical disadvantage meaningless. Today women can compete as well as men in the workforce.

5. "Woman was dethroned by the advent of private property, and her lot through the centuries has been bound up with private property." In order to bequeath the property, man wished to perpetuate the family and keep the patrimony, and he could do it only through the oppression of woman.

6. Christian ideology has contributed a great deal to the oppression of woman. In a religion that regards the flesh as accursed, woman symbolizes the devil's temptation and primal sin.

7. Man has always been creative and inventive: he "remodels the face of the earth, he creates new instruments, he invents, he shapes the future," while woman, being the victim of the species, has been destined for the repetitions of life.

8. Woman, having nothing to do, concentrates on her appearance and devotes her love to herself. Her appearance, unlike man's, is the reflection of her ego.

9. Woman does not act in accordance with her nature, but in accordance with man's expectations of her, "remodeled nearer to man's desire." Woman is largely man's invention.

10. Marriage is woman's traditional destiny: it is woman's biggest trap. Housework is empty, tedious, and monotonous. Motherhood mutilates woman. Liberation is possible for woman only outside marriage, while single.

11. To deny woman contraceptives and abortion is to deny her freedom and to make her a slave to her body.

12. The first step for liberation is for woman to have employment and be economically independent.

13. There is no female Shakespeare or female Dante because women have been denied access to the world and to diverse human experiences outside the home-conditions necessary for geniuses to flourish. Women have never had their chance in a world always dominated by men.

14. Love means different things for man and for woman. For woman, unlike man, love is an end in itself. Unable to assume responsibility for her life, woman relinquishes everything for the sake of a master. She attains a sense of herself only by serving.

15. The professional woman of today is torn among her professional interests as a human being, society's demands of her as a woman, and her sexual needs.

16. Woman's early education as a girl will always be against her even when she becomes a liberated and independent woman.

17. In the future, marriage should be between two independent human beings who recognize each other as equals. It will be an agreement based on liberty and honesty. Only then will men and women "affirm their brotherhood."

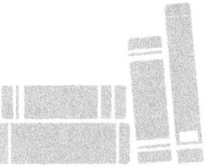

THE SECOND SEX

STRUCTURE, STYLE, SYNTAX

STRUCTURE

The Second Sex is divided into two books, seven parts, twenty-five chapters, an introduction, and a conclusion.

Each segment of *The Second Sex* follows, to a large extent, an academic form: the opening pages of each chapter present the **theme** in a quick succession of decisive and authoritative statements. The **theme** is often presented as an answer to a question. Then follow numerous examples and excerpts from books stitched together by commentary. The chapter ends in a summary of the main points and a restatement of ideas made throughout the chapter.

De Beauvoir presents her premises immediately in her introduction: women play a secondary role in a man-made society. Then in Book One, "Facts and Myths," Part I: "Destiny," she sets out to investigate the reasons for her basic premise from three points of view: biological, psychological, and historical materialism. Her conclusion: the reason for women's inferior condition is neither biological nor psychological but social; society is responsible for woman's secondary role.

In Part II: "History," de Beauvoir examines history to discover at what point and for what reasons society has assigned women a servile and passive role while man governs them. With numerous examples she establishes, first, that throughout history man has dominated woman; and second, that woman's enslavement began with the onset of private property.

If man has always dominated woman, what expectations has he of her? What role has she been expected to play? How well has she fitted into man's dreams and image of her? How have male writers depicted women in their books? The study of these questions constitutes Part III: "Myths."

Book Two is dedicated to the present: the condition of woman in contemporary society. In Parts IV and V de Beauvoir studies woman as girl, adolescent, bride, wife, mother, and grandmother, as well as lesbian and prostitute. In Part VI, de Beauvoir examines woman's options in a society that has always denied her the possibility to assert herself as a human being. Having no other way out, woman can justify her existence only in narcissism, in obsessive love, or in religion. In Part VII, de Beauvoir discusses the options currently open to the modern independent woman. Book Two concludes with the vision of a better and more just world in which men and women will not only be equal but also friends.

Method of Research

Simone de Beauvoir did her massive research exclusively in the library, and therefore all the support material and examples are secondary sources. Moreover, it seems that de Beauvoir's main thesis of the inferior condition of woman in a male-dominated world preceded her research, rather than being the result of her research, as it would be in a scientific study. Her method of proving her thesis was to call on other writers, historians, philosophers, and psychotherapists to prove her right. This method tends to be very subjective since de Beauvoir is naturally inclined to select those writers who agree with her. Consequently, much of her study, expressed in a very authoritative manner, frequently reflects de Beauvoir's personal opinion and feeling rather than an objective truth. Therefore, one should read the book with a critical eye and evaluate and weigh her arguments. This method of reading is not in itself negative, for it is better to read every book critically and not accept it blindly.

STYLE

De Beauvoir's subjective and personal style is at once her weakness and her strength: her weakness, since it tends to color facts and information her own way; her strength, since it creates a very personal **exposition** made of outpouring enthusiasm, angry criticism, decisive opinion, honest convictions, and passionate drive to unearth the truth. This high-pressure book is dense with stimulating arguments and provocative statements, packed with quotes and information. She is very decisive in her likes and dislikes and although they may often be debatable, they are always honest, lucid, and provocative. The merit of her ideas frequently lies not in their conclusions but in the stimulation they bring to the mind; their extremity urges the reader to think and take a stand.

Some critics have noted that de Beauvoir continues the tradition of the famous French moralists of the seventeenth and eighteenth centuries, religiously propounding her ideas in order to bring about change, believing in the possibility of creating a better world. Her contagious optimism, her bursting energy, her passionate affirmation of being and living make the reading of her book a joyous celebration.

But her enthusiasm is also responsible for the main weakness of her writing: excess. She never takes the short path to reach her point. She winds her way through excessively long sentences and lengthy paragraphs, mountains of information and endless quotations. Rather than selecting the strongest evidence, the most convincing data, she inundates the reader with every possible bit of information and idea. Her ardent desire to reach the truth, the whole truth, and all possible truths leads her to write down every argument for and against her thesis, even at the price of contradicting herself. Her almost compulsive need to leave nothing unsaid, no quote unmentioned, creates an unnecessarily long and cumbersome book. The serious readers who wish to follow her arguments may find themselves drowning in a flood of words; however, if the readers persist and persevere, they will surely be greatly rewarded.

De Beauvoir's style is uneven. While often vigorous and challenging, presenting crafted phrases and elegant sentence structure, it is also at times awkward and confusing. It is amazing that she could complete such a mammoth project in less than two-and-a-half years; but by the same token one wonders how much better the work could have been had she spent another two years sifting, editing, and chiseling it.

SYNTAX

De Beauvoir's long and winding sentences reflect the driving force of her restless mind: as her thoughts gush forward, her sentences stream on and on. She is fond of using the colon and especially the semicolon to punctuate so many of her sentences so she can continue her thoughts for a long while without stopping. Moreover, the colon and semicolon enable her to repeat and parallel her statements in endless variations, at times delightfully enriching her language in a rainbow of possibilities; at others, allowing her to repeat herself at annoying and tiresome length.

This parallel construction, which constitutes the majority of de Beauvoir's sentences, is a favorite of the Biblical prophets, the ancient moralists. In the Books of the Prophets, as in *The Second Sex*, parallelism appears in chiefly four forms:

1. Synonymous or repeating: one sentence or phrase is echoed by the next in different words:

Women inspire his books, feminine figures people them. (p. 269, Vintage Books edition, 1974)

This is what no woman has ever done, what none has been able to do. (p. 793)

In this penetration her inwardness is violated, she is like an enclosure that is broken into. (p. 24)

... he learns from an early age to take blows, to scorn pain, to keep back the tears. (p. 315)

2. Antithetic or contrasting: expressing a contrary thought.

For it is not in giving life but in risking life that man is raised above the animal; that is why superiority has been accorded in humanity not to the sex that brings forth but to that which kills. (p. 72)

> On the day when it will be possible for woman to love not in her weakness but in her strength, not to escape herself but to find herself; not to abase herself but to assert herself - on that day love will become for her, as for man, a source of life and not of mortal danger. (p. 743)

3. Complementary: the thought is completed by the following sentence or phrase:

> Now, woman has always been man's dependent, if not his slave: the two sexes have never shared the world in equality. (p. xxiv)

4. Climactic or ascending: where a word or a phrase in the first sentence is used as is, or in variation, in the second sentence, and the thought is then completed.

> . . . he prefers their love to any friendship, their friendship to that of men. (p. 269)

> It was as Mother that woman was fearsome; it is in maternity that she must be transfigured and enslaved. (p. 193)

This parallel construction allows poetic repetition, that is, repetition for the sake of the beauty and rhythm of the language rather than for the content. Here de Beauvoir is intoxicated with words, with their sensuous quality, their music and rhythm, and she enjoys making full use of them, a quality associated more with poetry than with critical writing. For example:

> ... sometimes in enmity, sometimes in amity, always in a state of tension. (p. 69)

> ... to maintain, he created; he burst out of the present, he opened the future. (p. 71)

Her intoxication with language is responsible for her rich vocabulary and beauty of language; but on the other hand, when overdone, for her exasperating verbosity.

Hers is a style of excess. She is prone to use emotionally loaded language when a simple phrase could suffice:

> ... he soars in the sky of heroes; woman crouches on earth beneath his feet. (p. 281)

> ... a woman is the trench into which he throws all the monsters that haunt him. (p. 282)

> **Woman is habituated to living on her knees. (p. 743)**

Carried away by her enthusiasm, de Beauvoir tends to serialize different parts of speech:

> nouns:... their dreams, their desires, their pleasures, their emotions, their ingenuities ... (p. 273)
>
> ... no law, no recipe, no reasoning, no example from without can any longer guide them. (p. 275)
>
> adjectives: ... she is cautious, hypocritical, play-acting .... (p. 293)
>
> ... most dubious, most poignant, most pungent ... (p. 274)
>
> ... partial, bruised, ridiculous, imperfect, mendacious forms. (p. 715)

verbs: ... the humane male also remodels ... creates ... invents ... shapes ... (p. 72)

infinitives: ... to lie to men, to scheme, to be wily ... (p. 292)

... to love not in her weakness but in her strength, not to escape herself but to find herself, not to abase herself but to assert herself ... (p. 742–3)

subordinate clauses: ... because the actress is at once judge and culprit, because she is her own dupe, because she imposes round-about ways ... (p. 276)

World of Absolutes

Simone de Beauvoir's world is one of certitude, of clearly defined borders, of absolutes; a world replete with "ever," "never," "always," "only," "very," "all," "must." Hers is not a Beckettian world of "maybe." Nothing is in confusion or in doubt. It is a world in black and white: "she is all that man desires and all that he does not attain." (p. 223) "Never have women constituted a separate caste, nor in truth have they ever as a sex sought to play a historic role." (p. 145) "This has always been a man's world." (p. 69).

Her extreme point of view is expressed by her choice of words: if she describes a woman's role as that of a "servant", being "oppressed" and "submissive," "always on her knees," she expresses a very definite and derogative point of view; it permits no dissent. But these same statements suggest their opposites: another author could have described a woman's role with just as much truth and conviction with words such as "nurturing," or "living for the good of others," "generous," "kind and soft," phrases that paint a diametrically different picture.

De Beauvoir's authority and confidence in the truth of her ideas, coupled with the beauty and rhythm of her language, naturally lead to the creation of many quotable sentences and delightful aphorisms to be found in almost every page.

To de Beauvoir's credit, one has to recognize that with her bold and direct use of language she has made the vocabulary of "femaleness" openly accepted in print and in speech. She has stripped once taboo words of female biology, such as "menstruation," "vagina," "clitoris," and even "pregnancy," of their traditional shame and made them a part of daily speech. The salvage of these words has brought female physiology and sexuality into legitimate existence.

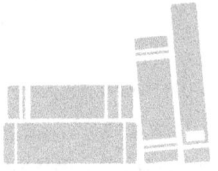

THE SECOND SEX

TEXTUAL ANALYSIS

INTRODUCTION

The Argument

"What is a woman?" asks Simone de Beauvoir and thus presents the main **themes** of the book:

1. While man sees himself as independent of woman, woman always sees herself in relation to man; while man is "essential," woman is "inessential"; while he is the "Subject," she is the "Other."

2. Women have always been subordinate to men and have never shared the world equally with them. Men are better off legally, economically, and politically: the world belongs to them.

Unlike other minorities such as Jews and Blacks, women cannot aspire to annihilate men, their oppressors, since there exists a special bond between them.

Commentary

From the start of her book, de Beauvoir shakes our accepted views of woman's role by questioning centuries-old ways of living. Aggressively and clearly she states her views, upsetting conventions, turning man-woman historical relationships inside out, questioning what men as well as women have always taken for granted.

De Beauvoir's technique is to ask provocative questions and then set out to answer them. In her responses she uses examples from history, philosophy, and literature, combined with commentary replete with authoritative and aggressive statements, such as "Yes, women on the whole are today inferior to men"; or, "Woman has always been man's dependent, if not his slave; the two sexes have never shared the world in equality," and even the most sympathetic of men will never be able to understand the profound negative and disabling effect, the stunting of creativity and activity, that this social discrimination has on woman.

In the introduction, de Beauvoir presents one of her basic concepts, that of the "Other," which involves the basic hostility that a person feels toward a stranger or a foreigner. This concept of "otherness" or "alienation" is central to the philosophy of existentialism: the conscious being is surrounded by a world of things, by impersonal institutions, and by complex technology that he cannot feel a part of and whose workings he cannot understand. Even more painful is his alienation from other human begins.

De Beauvoir extends the term of the "other" to the feeling of man toward woman: man sees woman not as a being like him but as the "other." Man, she claims, has never considered woman his peer, his friend, or his collaborator, but has treated her as one treats a stranger, and women submissively have accepted this role imposed on them by man.

The introduction ends with a series of poignant questions such as why, throughout history, women have been so submissive and subordinate, and how will they ever be able to overcome their obstacles and achieve independence and live like full human beings - questions that will take de Beauvoir 800 pages of small print to answer.

In her long and detailed response she investigates woman's role throughout history from the point of view of biology, psychoanalysis, and historical materialism; she studies woman's role as perceived by men and then by women; and lastly, she examines the ways women will be able to become human beings and assume their "full membership in the human race."

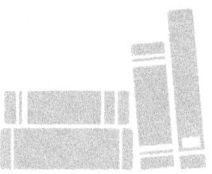

THE SECOND SEX

TEXTUAL ANALYSIS

BOOK ONE: FACTS AND MYTHS

PART I: DESTINY

Chapter I: The Data of Biology

The Argument

Not biology but society has made woman the second sex, submissive and inferior to man. Man has always perceived woman as the passive carrier and feeder of his seed, which is strong, active, and life-giving. But scientifically, egg and sperm are equally vital and active.

Woman's biological growth consists of crises; menstruation, pregnancy, childbirth, and menopause. Studying each crisis, de Beauvoir concludes that although woman is physically weaker than man, in a society that opposes violence and that relies on the machine to do the hard work, physical strength has little significance.

Commentary

This first chapter, which examines woman's biological makeup, was written at Sartre's suggestion, when de Beauvoir was already close to the end of her book. It is a theoretical and complicated chapter overburdened by numerous examples that appear unselectively in rapid succession and often obscure the writer's intention. The chapter's structure is based on drawing parallels between the development of reproduction in humans and in low high forms of animal life.

De Beauvoir's technique of describing at length the reproductive functions of animals and humans is very clinical, more befitting to a medical text than a philosophical study. For example, speaking about ovulation, she writes: "the follicle protrudes through the surface of the ovary and breaks open (sometimes with slight bleeding), the egg passes into the oviduct, and the wound develops into the corpus luteum." These long passages of technical descriptions make the text cumbersome and at times confusing.

De Beauvoir's examination of woman's biological development as a series of painful, unpleasant, and even depressing crises seems to be based on personal opinion, and one that many women would not share. Menstruation is "a burden," "distress causing," and "useless," as far as a woman is concerned. Likewise, pregnancy is "of no individual benefit to the woman," though it demands great sacrifices. Childbirth is painful and dangerous; nursing is tiring; menopause causes depression and other discomforts. Only after menopause can a woman relax from physical stress and be herself. Finally "she and her body are one."

The language de Beauvoir uses to describe these female crises is replete with negative words and phrases that evoke unpleasantness and disgust, and in a way, reflect man's negative view of female bodily functions rather than objective truth: "the bloody mass trickles," "debris escape," "wound," "breaks open." The discomfort and morning sickness of pregnancy is "the revolt of the organism against the invading species" that expresses the "infirmity in the abdomen"; and the fetus is a "hostile element," the result of "the species gnawing at their vitals," all phrases that express violence and repulsion.

De Beauvoir chose not to have children and never regretted her decision. Based on her own negative feeling toward pregnancy and raising children, she saw the female body not as an integral part of nature and not in harmony with the universe, but as alienated and burdensome. For her, a woman becomes an individual and a full human being when she acts against, not with, her physiology.

The Envious Male

It never occurred to de Beauvoir that woman's physiology and her biological function are beautiful and even enviable. Bruno Bettelheim in *Symbolic Wounds: Puberty Rites and the Envious Male* proves that parallel to what Freud called "penis envy" and "fear of castration" there exists a very strong wish on the part of the male to have female breasts, female reproductive organs, even to menstruate, and especially to be able to give birth. One may even come to the conclusion that this male envy of the woman's ability to create a human being is behind male aggressive activities, which are the object of de Beauvoir's admiration.

However, de Beauvoir is not always consistent and at times seems to be ambiguous about the issue of the female body. Twice toward the end of this chapter she mentions the importance of the body as "the instrument of our grasp upon the world," meaning that we understand the world through our body and our senses; she then writes that woman's biological functions affect her "central nervous system," a statement that shows the body to be of prime importance. At the same time, de Beauvoir's denial of the importance of the female functions creates a split between woman's mind and body. This will be a point of contention between de Beauvoir and the feminists who will strongly resent her low opinion of their bodies.

In spite of the discrepancies and ambiguities, de Beauvoir's conclusion of the chapter is insightful and valuable: woman's biological functions neither justify nor explain her passive existence and inferior status in society.

CHAPTER II: THE PSYCHOANALYTIC POINT OF VIEW

The Argument

De Beauvoir rejects Sigmund Freud's view on woman, claiming that he never dealt with woman's destiny but only applied his views on man to woman, assuming that woman feels like a mutilated man.

De Beauvoir agrees with Alfred Adler, who explained woman's inferiority complex as stemming not from lack of a penis but from her envying what it symbolizes: social superiority.

De Beauvoir argues that the young girl hesitates between being submissive and dependent as her education demands and being free and independent as she wishes. A woman should be defined as a "human being in quest of values in a world of values."

Commentary

De Beauvoir rightly points out that the great psychoanalysts were all men who did not concern themselves with, or could not really understand, the psychological makeup of a woman. For them man was an individual, but woman a "female." And whenever a woman behaved like a human being she was said to behave like a man. If Freud saw woman as a mutilated man, Adler, on the other hand, although his theories are closer to those of de Beauvoir's, could not conceive of a girl climbing trees as someone who likes to climb trees but as someone who wants to show off and prove she is equal to boys.

De Beauvoir argues with psychoanalytic theory on the issue of the individual's choice, a fundamental concept in existentialism. While psychoanalysts see the individual as being in the grip of his past, with his present determined by past events largely out of the individual's control, de Beauvoir, like Sartre - one of the originators of existentialism - strongly believes in the freedom of the individual to choose his destiny and create for himself the life he wishes to have. The idea of free choice is primary in *The Second Sex* and basic to de Beauvoir's general concept: every woman has the choice to free herself from the past, from society's derogatory views of her as inferior, and choose her freedom and independence, creating her present and future the way she wishes.

These are forceful and courageous statements in opposition to traditional and firmly rooted psychological ideas, and de Beauvoir is very convincing in her arguments against the all-powerful psychoanalysts of her time. Her views of free will attest to her unfailing optimism in the power of the individual - in this case woman - to be master of her own life.

De Beauvoir further develops her ideas about the education and the psychology of woman as a young girl and an adolescent in Part IV, "The Formative Years,"

> **CHAPTER III: THE POINT OF VIEW OF HISTORICAL MATERIALISM**

The Argument

Historical materialism postulates that to control nature one requires a strong hand to brandish a club and use instruments, and woman's physical weakness presents a "glaring inferiority." However, modern technology that needs little muscular strength may render woman man's equal.

According to Friedrich Engels, when people lived a communal life, woman played a large role in the economic life of her society, but with the discovery of metals and the invention of the plow, woman's muscular weakness rendered her inferior. Man became the proprietor of land and also of woman.

Still, de Beauvoir claims, the association of man and woman could be friendly. Not ownership itself, but man's inherent drive for power and enrichment made him enslave woman, binding her to maternity.

Commentary

In her relentless effort to prove that man has always been unjust to woman, de Beauvoir skillfully questions existing theories to show that even such great scholars and theoreticians as Freud, Adler, and Engels misunderstood, minimized, or simply did not take into consideration woman's complex situation. Her reasoning is solid, as she firmly outlines the differences between conditions for men and for women, even though she may take a long and winding road to explain her views.

Although de Beauvoir agrees with Engels that the passage from the community to private ownership brought about the oppression of woman and constitutes a historical turning point, she courageously denounces him for not explaining how this situation came about, formulating her own theory: (1) The institution of private property was made possible only by the enslavement of women. (2) It is not private property itself but the "imperialism of human consciousness" that made man enslave woman. (3) To dominate her, man destined woman to a life of maintaining the home, giving birth, and raising his children. (4) With birth control, abortion, and divorce prohibited, as they are prohibited in all patriarchal societies, woman remained a slave to man.

Part I of *The Second Sex*, the study of woman from three different points of view - biological, psychoanalytical, and historical materialist - is greatly influenced by Sartre's philosophical study *Being and Nothingness* (1943), which may be summed up as a defense of freedom as the essential characteristic of human beings: it is free will and not determinism that governs our destiny. Our past, as Freud claimed, and our social class-conflict, as Marx theorized, do not control our life; we are free to make our own choices. Although the facts of life - our biological, psychological, sociological, and economic situation - are important, we, as conscious beings, can choose the meaning these facts have for us. It is we who give meaning to the facts.

Thus de Beauvoir has applied Sartre's thinking to her study of woman. In the conclusion of the first part of *The Second Sex*, she emphatically states that neither woman's biology, nor psychoanalysis, nor historical materialism sufficiently and satisfactorily explain woman's inferior condition. In order to be able to explain it, de Beauvoir feels that she has to reach beyond them, and so she takes a journey into history that will constitute the second part of *The Second Sex*.

PART II: HISTORY

Chapter IV: The Nomads

The Argument

"This has always been a man's world," declares de Beauvoir, while women, being often pregnant and unable to provide for all their offspring, passively submitted to their biological destiny, bound to the repetition of life.

Man, creative and inventive, was engaged in harnessing nature and shaping the future. And as value was placed on creation and not on repetition, woman was at a great disadvantage.

Commentary

De Beauvoir opens this chapter in her usual way, with an authoritative statement, and then proceeds as if her original premise is an unrefuted truth. However, this has not always been a man's world, claim some contemporary anthropologists and feminist scholars who base their studies on recent archeological findings and new researches that reveal signs of an ancient goddess-worshiping period and of matriarchal societies.

From the very beginning of history, de Beauvoir says, men had the creative and adventurous jobs, while women were relegated to repetitious work. This seems to contradict what she says in the previous chapter, that in the Stone Age, when people lived in a communal environment, there was equality between the sexes; while men hunted and fished, women made pottery, wove and gardened, and played "a large part in economic life."

In this chapter de Beauvoir tends to repeat some previously stated ideas about man's muscular strength and woman's lack of it. But she manages to repeat her ideas in a very stylistic and elegant way that calls for our appreciation. Her statements are so well-chiseled and crystal-clear that they would find a place of honor in any quotation book.

She expresses ideas, which are often unconventional and insightful, in piercing and commanding aphorisms: "Man's design is not to repeat himself in time: it is to take control of the instant and mold the future." Or, "It is male activity that in creating values has made of existence itself a value."

In her first step into the beginning of human society, de Beauvoir looks for an answer to one of her basic questions: what gave man superiority over woman? And again she concludes that man's physical strength made all the difference: while woman stayed close to home, man dared to go out into the world, be adventurous, risk his life and become a hero, returning home proud of his achievements. Woman was excluded from all these experiences. And here de Beauvoir offers one of her most original observations of human society:

"... it is not in giving life but in risking life that man is raised above the animal; that is why superiority has been accorded in humanity not to the sex that brings forth but to that which kills."

CHAPTER V: EARLY TILLERS OF THE SOIL

The Argument

Land ownership required that you have children to bequeath the land to, and thus motherhood became sacred. This has created the myth that once there existed female rule. In fact, women were always under the guardianship of males - father, brother, or husband. Their role was to serve, never to create.

The reasons for this situation are two: (1) Woman did not share man's way of working and was excluded from mastering land and inventing tools. (2) Woman's reproductive function remained connected to the mysterious process of life, and therefore man never considered her a partner. In making children his own, man dominated the world and woman. And when man learned to write, he wrote the laws.

Commentary

In this chapter de Beauvoir attempts to prove what she says in her chapter on "Historical Materialism," that woman's historical defeat came with the advent of agriculture and private property.

De Beauvoir's statement that woman was excluded from the creative process of inventing tools is being contested by contemporary scholars who are crediting women with the invention of pottery, textiles, construction, cooking, planting, and milling.

De Beauvoir refutes the existence of a matriarchate, a period of history when women ruled. However, since the publication of *The Second Sex*, and often inspired by it, many feminist scholars have researched the past and often arrived at different conclusions. Many insist that women did enjoy a "Golden Age of Woman," that there was a period of matriarchate when women ruled and determined the values of society. Other scholars, using recently discovered archeological data, agree with de Beauvoir that in prehistoric society matriarchy did not exist, but they stress that the opposite-male rule - did not exist either. They claim that prehistoric society was remarkably equalitarian. And although descent appears to have been traced through the mother, and women served as priestesses, heads of clans, and played leading roles in all aspects of life, there is no indication that men were subordinate (E. G. Davis, *The First Sex* [1971]; M. Stone, *When God was a Woman* [1978]; R. Eisler, *The Chalice and the Blade* [1987]).

CHAPTER VI: PATRIARCHAL TIMES AND CLASSICAL ANTIQUITY

The Argument

For centuries woman was reduced to being a part of man's property. In antiquity, among the Arabs, the Hebrews, the Moslems, the Babylonians, and the Persians, woman was the absolute property of man, her life literally in his hands. Polygamy, allowed for man, was strictly forbidden for woman, mainly to insure the transference of his property to his children. Only in Egypt, Sparta, and Rome did women enjoy some rights.

Commentary

In this chapter de Beauvoir reaches two of her most important conclusions concerning the condition of woman:

(1) Throughout history woman's destiny had been "bound up with private property." Woman's oppression lay in man's desire to enlarge and perpetuate his property so that he could bequeath it to his children. Woman's sole hope for liberty had been outside the family and marriage. She could, however, enjoy some freedom in Egypt or in Sparta, where there was no private property, or in Greece as a courtesan.

(2) Legal rights, or "abstract rights," were not enough to make women free. Even when women gained legal rights, as in Rome, they still remained in a state of slavery unless they gained economic independence: it is woman's economic independence that brings her liberty.

This chapter is strong proof of de Beauvoir's basic postulate that from the beginning of history, woman, devoid of human rights and dignity, was a second-class citizen in the service of man, being more of a slave than a person, merely a part of his property, and her life completely at his mercy. Customs and laws meant one thing for males and another for females: a woman's life and value were taken lightly. Among the Arabs, for example, it was an act of generosity for a father to accept the female child and not kill her; the Hebrews reduced a man's punishment if the victim was female; the Muslims extolled the superiority of man as God-given.

One surprising discussion is de Beauvoir's analysis of man's demand for woman to be chastised, not for the sake of morality but for the preservation of private property. While man could take as many wives as he could afford, he wanted at the same time to insure that his property would pass on to his children proper, and not to those fathered by a stranger, so he ruled that wives should be strictly chastised for adultery. The Biblical patriarchs, for example, had several wives, while the Hebrew law required an adulterous wife to be stoned to death.

In this grim reality, Egypt and Sparta seem like rays of light: they treated their woman almost as equal to man, only because having no private property, man did not need woman as an instrument to bear him children to whom to bequeath his property. In Egypt all land belonged to the king; in Sparta there was a communal regime, and all children belonged to the community: adultery disappeared with the disappearance of patrimony.

Only outside marriage and family life, concludes de Beauvoir, did woman have a chance to be a full human being. The Greek courtesans, free from the obligations of marriage and child bearing, attained the rank of human beings: they were free to develop their personality, talents, intellectual, and artistic ability, with many of them gaining celebrity, riches, and power. The courtesan Lamia was a perfect example. This is true not only of women of antiquity but also of contemporary women, as de Beauvoir will explain in the second part of *The Second Sex*. It is certainly amazing and convincing to see what women can achieve once they are free to try.

De Beauvoir uses the complex condition of woman in Rome to prove that having legal rights means little if women lack economic independence and political power to make use of these rights. Beginning in the year 178 A.D., mothers and daughters were legally equal to fathers and sons, but the Senate issued a law forbidding women to enter into contracts with other citizens, thus depriving women of almost every legal capability and of exercising the rights they had gained.

This chapter attests to de Beauvoir's excellent research skills in gathering examples to prove her points. Her weakness lies not in bringing too few examples, but, absurdly enough, in bringing too many, so that the reader is submerged in and stupefied by her erudition. However, one must admit that she has unearthed revealing and certainly convincing facts about women and their complex relationship with men in classical antiquity.

CHAPTER VII: THROUGH THE MIDDLE AGES TO EIGHTEENTH-CENTURY FRANCE

The Argument

"Christian ideology has contributed no little to the oppression of woman," declares Simone de Beauvoir. In a religion that views the flesh as a curse, woman becomes the symbol of the devil's temptation. Although the Bible extends some charity to women as to lepers, St. Paul's subordination of women to men is based solidly on the Old and New Testaments.

In the Middle Ages, the European legal codes were all unfavorable to women who lived in a state of slavery. This remained largely unchanged until the nineteenth century.

However, during the Renaissance, some bright women, by becoming courtesans, acquired powerful positions. Such positions were unavailable for the majority of women, but some of the wealthy, intelligent, and ambitious ones enjoyed some freedom.

Commentary

It is during the Renaissance that for the first time de Beauvoir finds some women worthy of her praise. She admires those female achievers who successfully entered the world of men. Because the Renaissance encouraged individualism, some women managed to avoid a woman's lot by escaping marriage and becoming courtesans, free in spirit and finances, studying philosophy and science, and setting up laboratories for the study of physics and chemistry. Several rose to prominence and became powerful rulers, soldiers and leaders, artists, writers and musicians. Examples include Mme. de Sevigne (1626–96), who was a widow when she wrote her celebrated letters, and Mme. de Pompadour (1721–64), the powerful mistress of Louis XV of France. This proves that under favorable conditions, with money and with no man to hinder them, women could be creative and active and proud of their achievements. Yet, none of these women became a Dante or a Shakespeare!

Here, de Beauvoir is touching on one of the most poignant issues concerning woman's secondary role in society: Where is the female Dante, the she-Shakespeare? Well, there is none, admits de Beauvoir, and offers two reasons for that unfortunate fact. One, lack of female education, and especially so for the masses of women, for after all, according to de Beauvoir, "it is often from the mass that masculine genius has arisen.... while nothing hindered the flights of a St. Theresa or a Catherine the Great, a thousand circumstances conspired against the woman writer." Only in the eighteenth century was there a middle-class woman, a widow, Aphra Behn, who earned a living by her writing. The second reason is that women never enjoyed the material independence necessary for inner liberty, a requisite for every writer.

De Beauvoir, who never takes a short cut when writing, dedicates only half a page to answer such a disturbing and prevalent question so often used nowadays to prove woman's inferiority. Her answer is surprisingly shallow and unsatisfying, especially coming from such an analytical and sharp mind as hers. The two reasons she offers are not convincing and even seem to contradict each other. Genius writers, she postulates, arise from the mass; and geniuses need economic independence to have inner liberty. But it is the mass that, more often than not, lacks financial independence, and, having to struggle for mere survival, has no time and no inner liberty at all. In the following chapter, however, de Beauvoir addresses this controversial issue again, and her answer is far more convincing.

CHAPTER VIII: SINCE THE FRENCH REVOLUTION - THE JOB AND THE VOTE

The Argument

The French Revolution did not change the lives of women, although some women gained celebrity, e.g., Charlotte Corday, who assassinated Marat and influenced history, and Olympe de Gouges, who proposed a "Declaration of the Rights of Woman" (1789) and died on the guillotine. During Napoleon's military dictatorship only unmarried woman enjoyed full civil power.

Significant change came with the Industrial Revolution. The advent of the machine opened for women a new era and new possibilities: it destroyed (1) "landed property," and (2) the physical advantage men had over women. Escaping from the kitchen to the factory, women achieved economic importance. They began to organize, demonstrate, and strike, demanding full political rights that they won in America in 1920, in England in 1928, and in France in 1945. But it is in the Soviet Union where women made the most progress.

Commentary

In this very long chapter which is overburdened by details, de Beauvoir attempts to prove that history never gave women the chance to fully be themselves. Even great historical events such as the French Revolution, which was meant to liberate mankind, did not include women's rights on their agenda. Only when women gained economic independence, as in the Industrial Revolution, did they begin to fight for their rights as human beings, and when they did, they largely succeeded.

De Beauvoir argues with the great theoreticians of the time, Marx and Engels, who did not address themselves to the emancipation of woman assuming, mistakenly, that the liberation of the working class would naturally include the liberation of women. But, de Beauvoir claims, both Marx and Engels ignored or misunderstood woman's complex condition as woman and as worker: (1) Female workers were more exploited than men and earned half their pay, although women often did better work. (2) Women did not know how to organize and defend themselves to improve horrifying working conditions. Years of submission and resignation had resulted in lack of solidarity and collective consciousness. Only in 1874 did the law intervene to limit the work load of minor female workers, and later it even allowed women some rights. (3) One of woman's greatest problems has always been the reconciliation of motherhood and work, especially when contraception and abortion are unavailable.

WOMEN IN HISTORY

Surveying history, de Beauvoir reaches the following conclusions expressed in some of her celebrated aphorisms: (1) "The whole of feminine history has been man-made." (2) Only very few women have protested against their destiny, but on the whole "men have always held the lot of woman in their hands" and the majority of women were resigned to their destiny. (3) Women have never even tried to play a historical role. Even singular women, like Joan of Arc, are "exemplary figures rather than historical agents." Women exist "on the margin of history."

Some feminists, notably Margaret Simons, have openly accused the English translator of *The Second Sex*, H. M. Parshley, of distorting de Beauvoir's presentation of women in history by cutting about 300 pages from the original French, including stories and names of 78 women in history; as a result, de Beauvoir's rendering of the passive role of women in history becomes exaggerated in the English edition. Margaret Simons plans to publish the missing parts. However, other feminists, such as Mary Lowenthal Felstiner, have complained that their main problem with *The Second Sex* is its unmanageable proportions, being "too long and too hard" as it is.

Great Women

De Beauvoir argues with the antifeminists who declare contradictorily that (1) "women have never created anything great"; and (2) "the situation of women never prevented the flowering of great feminine personalities." Her answer is lucid and encompassing: The success of a few great women does not excuse the abuse of the many, and the very fact that so few great women existed only proves the unfavorable condition of woman. Simply put, "In no domain has woman ever really had her chance."

Here, de Beauvoir resumes her discourse from the previous chapter concerning the lack of women geniuses. Consistent with her existentialist philosophy, she says that people are not born what they are, but they become who they are in accordance with their status and environment; likewise, "one is not born a genius: one becomes a genius" and in order to become a genius, one needs favorable conditions, something women have never had.

Structure

The organization of the chapter leaves much to be desired. Piling up too many details and endless examples, de Beauvoir obscures rather than clarifies her main idea. Information is important, but indiscriminate accumulation of information brings about the opposite result, and in this chapter one can easily become lost. Editing, sifting, and selecting the historical data, as well as highlighting the connection between each detail and the entire picture would have worked wonders. One needs much patience to dig through de Beauvoir's crowded and intense style to find the jewels in the heap of words; but jewels they are, and one is occasionally rewarded with clear, authoritative statements that demonstrate just how original, provocative, and insightful de Beauvoir can be. These statements, and there are quite a few of them in this chapter, are quotable and could be used as banners in women's struggle for liberation and equality. And even if one disagrees with a particular statement such as "one is not born a genius: one becomes a genius," one has to admit that it is thought-provoking.

The second part of *The Second Sex*, "History," is one of Simone de Beauvoir's greatest contributions to culture. For the very first time woman is provided with her own history. De Beauvoir makes woman existent in a history that has, until recently, little place for her: history has been mostly of men, written by men. By providing woman with a history, de Beauvoir evokes woman's consciousness of herself, spurring her to question the role history, society, and man have assigned her.

The end of Part II brings us to the middle of the twentieth century, with de Beauvoir having completed her detailed survey of woman's condition throughout history. Because her conclusion is that throughout history women have been, and still are, largely submissive, the unfortunate and very damaging result is that women make their choices not in accordance with their own nature but in accordance with man's expectations of them; women see themselves not as they are but as men see them. Therefore, the third part of *The Second Sex* will be a study of woman as man sees her.

PART III: MYTHS

Chapter IX: Dreams, Fears, Idols

The Argument

Man's myths of woman are contradictory: she is at once Eve and the Virgin Mary, an idol and a servant, good and evil, life and death. He is mystified, both attracted and horrified by menstruation, virginity, childbirth, and motherhood. He dreams to control and possess woman, to shape her to fit his dreams, while woman tries hard to live up to his dreams of her.

Commentary

Never before has a scholar presented so strong an indictment of society's accepted view of woman. Never before has this traditional view been probed so thoroughly. De Beauvoir's revolutionary concept concludes that what we commonly know of woman is not what woman really is, but it is man's image of her, a reflection of his fantasies and of his nightmares; and that woman, on the other hand, has accepted these dreams, trying hard to live up to them. Instead of having a life of her own, she has been living only in relation to man, a heroine in the myths he has invented.

This study of the myths men have created around women was de Beauvoir's starting point in writing *The Second Sex*, and here she is at her best. Even though she is still taking the long route to prove her point, that route is teeming with many interesting conclusions and quotable statements of profound insight. With only a few words, she is able to throw light on entire social or psychological situations:

The ideal of the average Western man is a woman who freely accepts his domination, who does not accept his ideas without but who yields to his arguments, who resists him intelligently and ends by being convinced.

Her conclusions on love are equally insightful: "... this struggle remain[s] a game for him, while for woman it involves her very destiny." And, "... eroticism implies a claim of the instant against time."

This study of woman as man's invention, of man imposing his image on woman, and of woman, who instead of living her own life, submissively lives up to man's image of her, is one of de Beauvoir's most original chapters. She throws light on areas never before analyzed so deeply from a woman's point of view: man's ambivalent attitude toward menstruation, childbirth, mother, mother-in-law, the Virgin Mary, and his own sexuality.

Even costumes, jewelry, and makeup are but means to remodel woman to resemble man's dream of her, to control her body and to prevent her from being just what she is, a human being. The following example demonstrates how insightful, succinct, and precise de Beauvoir can be:

> **Chinese women with bound feet could scarcely walk, the polished fingernails of the Hollywood star deprive her of her hands; high heels, corsets .... were intended less to accentuate the curves of the feminine body than to augment its incapacity. Weighted down with fat, or on the contrary so thin as to forbid all effort, paralyzed by inconvenient clothing and by the rules of propriety - then woman's body seems to man to be his property, his thing.**

Often compared to water, woman reflects man's image: when he looks at her he wishes to see himself as virile, as hero, or as victim.

De Beauvoir takes man's view of woman a step further into abstraction, and brilliantly demonstrates how man has spiritualized woman as soul, idea, Muse - necessary for his creativity, but never creative herself. As idol or witch, from man's point of view, woman is never an individual, but a creature tailor-made to his complex and contradictory dreams of her. And faithfully woman plays the part man expects of her:

she dreams "through the dreams of men," while in his dreams of himself as a hero, he has assigned her only a secondary role.

If de Beauvoir's view of man is negative, her view of woman is even more so. De Beauvoir's woman is depicted as a total mindless victim who accepts unquestioningly, even with dedication, man's view of her, and as a puppet does her best to serve his dreams. Has woman really been so mindless a victim, such a puppet throughout history? When a woman dresses up, wears jewelry and makeup, could it be that she enjoys doing so?

CHAPTER X: THE MYTH OF WOMAN IN FIVE AUTHORS

The Argument

Simone de Beauvoir studies the works of five noted writers to prove the validity of her analysis of the way men perceive women.

1. Montherlant or the bread of disgust. Henry de Montherlant's views of woman are extremely negative: women are stupid, ignorant, and illogical; the mother mutilates her son, the mistress hinders her man, both only take and do not give. The ideal woman is stupid and submissive, purely flesh, "an object to be enjoyed."

2. D. H. Lawrence or phallic pride. Although it seems that Lawrence advocates the equality of the sexes, in truth he believes in the inherent power of the male principle: the phallus will bring the two sexes together. Lawrence's men are active, his women passive, the wife derives her fulfillment from her husband.

3. Claudel and the handmaid of the Lord. Paul Claudel, a devout Catholic, believes that through the temptation of Eve and subsequent ruin, man will become aware of his soul and win salvation. In a more poetic and modernized form, Claudel expresses the Catholic tradition: woman's destiny is to dedicate herself to family and Church.

4. Breton or poetry. For Andre Breton woman has no vocation other than love. She is poetry and the key to the beyond, she is all-except herself.

5. Stendhal or the romantic of reality. Stendhal is a true "tender friend of women" as they really are. He accuses men of depriving women of opportunities and providing them with inferior education. Because they are oppressed, women are free of man's pursuit of profit and are free to be true to themselves.

Commentary

De Beauvoir demonstrates how the myth of woman plays a significant role in the literature of male writers. She analyzes in great detail the writing and characters of five male writers, four French and one English, displaying analytical power and psychological insight as well as a wide knowledge of literature. This has prompted some critics to consider this chapter as the most brilliant in *The Second Sex*.

It is also the first time that de Beauvoir, often criticized for her lack of humor, demonstrates her talent for **satire**, especially in the section on de Montherlant. She mocks his arrogance, calling him "a specialist in heroism" who wishes to "dethrone" woman. "He believes he is God, he wants to be God; and this because he is male, because he is a 'superior man,' because he is de Montherlant."

De Montherlant, according to de Beauvoir, is a true woman-hater who dislikes woman in any role - as mother, mistress, or idol. With psychological insight she offers an original interpretation of his negative attitude to women: it stems not from his knowledge of women, but from his own arrogance, from his resentment and anger toward his mother who gave birth to a human being and not to God, as he wished to be.

Although D. H. Lawrence is commonly considered a champion of women, Simone de Beauvoir proves that he, too, believes in the supremacy of the male, expecting his intelligent women to recognize this fact.

Stendhal: A True Feminist

De Beauvoir considers Stendhal the only one of the five male authors to be a genuine friend of woman and to acknowledge woman as a person. De Beauvoir shares Stendhal's admiration for his heroines, who, although weak and dependent, are superior human beings because they, unlike his men, are guided by their moral understanding, recognizing that the true values are those of the heart. De Beauvoir hails him for being able to perceive woman as just a woman, neither good nor evil, neither an idol nor a witch, neither poetry nor temptation, and as a woman of flesh and blood, worth more than man's dream of her.

Only Stendhal, says de Beauvoir, recognizes the wrongs society has done to woman by depriving her of her potential. He too deals with the controversial question of why there is not a female Dante or a female Shakespeare and aggressively accuses society for the lack of women geniuses. De Beauvoir quotes him with delight: "All geniuses who are born women are lost to the public welfare; once fate gives them means to make themselves known, you will see them achieve the most difficult attainments." This study of Stendhal, whom de Beauvoir calls a feminist, is the most lucid and best organized of the five.

The first four male writers adequately illustrate the thesis of de Beauvoir's preceding chapter that man, unable to see woman as a simple human being, has created different and often contradictory myths around her. On the other hand, the fact that one male writer out of five is a woman's friend is encouraging. Moreover, in the next chapter, de Beauvoir mentions two other French writers who seem to be devout feminists. That brings the number of women's friends among the male writers to three, and three friends out of seven suggests that maybe Simone de Beauvoir exaggerates, and men are not completely hopeless as far as women are concerned.

CHAPTER XI: MYTH AND REALITY

The Argument

The myth surrounding women is so powerful that even contrary facts seem impotent to disprove it. The reasons man has created this myth instead of seeing woman as she is are: (1) Man defines woman by her group and not by her individuality. (2) The myth justifies the privileges and abuse of the ruling class. (3) It provides easy explanations for what seems inexplicable in a woman. (4) Like all oppressed people, women have become conditioned to lie, to scheme, to play-act, to wear a mask. The time has come, declares de Beauvoir, to discard the myth of woman and recognize in her the human being.

Commentary

In this chapter de Beauvoir again begins with questions and then tries to answer them. Her answers comprise a relatively short, concisely and clearly written chapter, in which she calls for the abolition of the false and unfair myth of woman and for the emergence of woman as an independent individual responsible not for her traditional feminine role but for her own actions and behavior.

The split between reality and the myth of woman is so deep that it makes it very difficult for the modern woman to accept both her independence and her feminine destiny at the same time. The tension between the two creates in woman so much anguish and restlessness that she may give up and conclude that it is easier to submit "to blind enslavement than to work for liberation."

At the same time that de Beauvoir calls for the abolition of the myth of woman, she displays an understanding of the importance of myth and dreams in a person's life. And so to those who fear that without the myth man will be robbed of his dreams and of his creativity, and that the relationship between man and woman will be devoid of their magic, she says:

To discard the myth is not to destroy all dramatic relation between the sexes ... it is not to do away with poetry, love, adventure happiness, dreaming. It is simply to ask that behavior, sentiment, passion be founded upon the truth.

To support her ideas, de Beauvoir uses inspiring quotes by two male French writers, Laforgue and Rimbaud. Laforgue prays for women to be "our brothers in intimacy," and Rimbaud calls for women to be free and themselves. These feminist quotes, as well as her previously expressed admiration for Stendhal, provide a counter-argument to her own denigration of male writers. It is interesting that the only feminist quotes de Beauvoir offers are from male writers. Does it mean that male writers are more feminist than women writers? Or that de Beauvoir has more respect for male writers, and in their writings is looking for affirmation of her ideas?

This chapter ends the first book of *The Second Sex*. After discussing the "Destiny," "History," and "Myths" of woman, de Beauvoir is ready to embark on the study of the contemporary woman, which will constitute the second book.

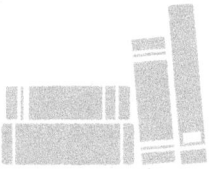

THE SECOND SEX

BOOK TWO: WOMAN'S LIFE TODAY

PART IV: THE FORMATIVE YEARS

Chapter XII: Childhood

The Argument

"One is not born, but rather becomes a woman," declares de Beauvoir. Female destiny is imposed on woman by society. Boys and girls are raised differently: boys to be active; girls to be passive and repress their impulses.

Girls are raised in a man-made world: the songs, legends, and mythology present men as heroes. In religion, they are presented as superiors: God, Christ, Pope, and priest; the only notable woman in Christianity, The Virgin Mary, kneels before her son.

In puberty, too, the girl's experience is radically different from the boy's: her body becomes "an object destined for another." Society expects her to be "pure" and "innocent" just when she is discovering her sexuality.

Commentary

De Beauvoir opens the first chapter on the "formation" of woman with one of her most quoted aphorisms, that a woman is not born a woman-meaning, she is not born different from man or inferior to him, but she is made so by society. However, today the same statement may be given a different interpretation; i.e., that one is not born a woman but creates herself a woman, that one has a choice of being fulfilled as a woman - as a full human being who is endowed, not burdened, with female characteristics such as nurturing, kindliness, gentility, or peace lovingness. One becomes a woman by choice, different from man but by no means inferior. This interpretation suits the modern liberated woman, as it hands free will back to her, and turns de Beauvoir's passive woman into an active person.

Today, nearly 40 years after *The Second Sex* was published, and largely as a result of its publication, de Beauvoir's recounting of the formation of little girls seems overstated and dated. Fortunately we are a long way from the time when girls were utterly surprised and shocked at their first menstruation. Girls today await the onset of menstruation with expectation, viewing it as a sign of maturity, are proud of it and talk about it openly even in front of men. This does not mean that we have reached a sexually egalitarian society, but that we are closer to it today - no doubt with the help of *The Second Sex* - than when de Beauvoir was a child.

This very long chapter is a compilation of insightful analysis, sound common sense, incisive aphorisms, tiring repetitions and abundant exaggerations. De Beauvoir not only repeats much of what she has said in previous chapters but also argues every side of every question, quoting lavishly and at length from women's biographies psychological studies, and case histories.

CHAPTER XIII: THE YOUNG GIRL

The Argument

Not by developing herself as a human being but by "modeling herself upon their dreams" does the adolescent girl gain value in men's eyes. She learns that to be feminine is to appear weak and docile. She is torn between her natural impulse to be free and active and the social demands on her to be "feminine" and passive. Mothers, often hostile to their daughters' liberation, curtail their freedom and overburden them with housework. Today the adolescent girl has the alternative of taking her future into her own hands, engaging in studies, sports, or politics.

Commentary

Many contemporary young women will find it hard to identify with de Beauvoir's portrayal of the adolescent girl, though their mothers or grandmothers may see themselves expressed in this portrayal.

De Beauvoir views boys' aggressive activities, such as climbing trees and fighting peers, as building and strengthening their personality. However, she cannot imagine that girls' activities, such as picking wild flowers, jumping rope, or just quietly observing life, can also be strengthening to one's individuality. The young girls of *The Second Sex* are often neurotic, maladjusted, raging at their mothers, who are vengeful and equally frustrated and neurotic.

On the whole de Beauvoir seems to overstate her ideas of women's woes, claiming that women in general are prone to neuroses, disorders, and nightmares, all as a result of having to cope in a man-made society. One wishes that de Beauvoir had not made women seem such complete victims, devoid of all intelligence and aspirations, becoming only play-dolls in men's hands.

A Partial View

Even if we accept de Beauvoir's thesis that women, dominated by men, play only a secondary role in society, we may wonder: (1) Is it possible that women may have willingly accepted their role because they do not find it as horrendous as de Beauvoir presents it? (2) Is it possible that women find their role to be nurturing and not subservient, and rewarding in a way de Beauvoir cannot grasp because of her particular experiences and makeup? (3) Is it possible that women may actually be as men see them - without sufficient intelligence to develop themselves within their existing limitations, or to turn those limitations into advantages? Although there is much truth in de Beauvoir's analysis and conclusions about the condition of woman, one wonders if her view is only part of the truth.

Once again de Beauvoir refers to female biological functions with negative expressions: menstruation is always painful and loathsome and breasts are burdensome. Words such as "prey," "nightmare," "stifling," "rape," and "passivity" abound in relation to women. To be feminine, for de Beauvoir is to accept defeat. Even Stendhal, who is hailed by de Beauvoir as a champion of woman, has found in the Otherness of woman not only the advantage of avoiding many of man's dismal qualities but also her being an outsider, an observer who is better able to judge true human values. But de Beauvoir finds nothing, absolutely nothing redeeming or beautiful in woman as she is.

CHAPTER XIV: SEXUAL INITIATION

The Argument

The first sexual experience for man and woman is utterly different, biologically, socially, and psychologically, according to de Beauvoir. For the girl it is often unexpected and disagreeable, "an act of violence," a break with the past.

The sexual act ends with male's satisfaction, whereupon the female's "service to the species begins," slowly and painfully, in pregnancy, birth, and child-raising. Woman has been restricted to marriage and chastity while man's sexual freedom has been taken for granted.

Commentary

This chapter is a brilliant study of the biological and psychological dissimilarities of man and woman in the shared sexual act. With profound insight and verbal daring, de Beauvoir gives words to experiences and feelings that have for long remained nameless. She is especially successful when she describes in minute detail the various psychological stages a woman experiences before and during the sexual act. Even today, in an age of permissiveness and sexual frankness, this chapter's exploration of human sexuality can teach both women and men about each other.

Here, too, in the domain of sexuality often kept quiet, de Beauvoir boldly calls for equality and partnership between the sexes. She argues strongly against the prevalent view, held also by some psychoanalysts, that women do feel the desire to be dominated in the sexual act and that this masochistic feeling is characteristic of females. This may be true only in abnormal cases, de Beauvoir says. For woman to achieve full sexual pleasure she requires love and affection. Only then will woman overcome her passivity and become a partner to her man. The difference between the eroticism of man and woman is apparent only when the sexual act is a battle, and it can be easily solved if the man expresses his desire and respect, and recognizes woman's freedom.

However, some parts in this chapter, as well as in her first chapter, "The Data of Biology," have justly aroused much resentment among women. Many feminists have taken issue with de Beauvoir on what they have perceived as de Beauvoir's negative and even repulsive attitude toward female anatomy. In both chapters de Beauvoir uses derogatory and strongly unpleasant words whenever she describes female sex organs. While she describes the male's organ as "simple and neat as a finger" and "readily visible", the female's is "concealed, mucous, and humid ... it bleeds each month ... often sullied with body fluids." This description is likely to be more a man's view of a woman's body than a woman's. In particular, her **metaphor** of the feminine sex desire as "the soft throbbing of a mollusk" drew hostile criticism, as did the following quote:

woman lies in wait like the carnivorous plant, the bog, in which insects and children are swallowed up. She is absorption, suction, humus, pitch and glue, a passive influx, insinuating and viscous.

Some feminists claim that (1) de Beauvoir describes her personal disgust of her own body, and that this feeling of disgust is by no means common to all women; (2) she could not conceive that women may feel in total harmony with their bodies and even be proud of them, just as a male is proud of his; and (3) she has accepted women's sexual passivity as a biological fact without understanding that women can be naturally as active and sexually aggressive as men.

The section about the threat of pregnancy, which paralyzes a woman's sexual desire, emphasizes, when read today, the degree of progress Western society has undergone since the publication of *The Second Sex*. During the past forty years, with medical advances that have made contraception safer and easier to obtain and to use, women have gained much control over their reproductive system. The increased availability of contraception is, as de Beauvoir has rightly claimed, a great step in the emancipation of women.

CHAPTER XV: THE LESBIAN

The Argument

Some women who refuse to be a sexual object and who reject the inferior and passive feminine role society has imposed on them, or those who seek to cultivate their feminity in "masculine freedom," may choose homosexuality. There are many lesbians among women artists and writers, not because their sexual tendency is the source of creativity, but because they are too absorbed in their work to have the time for the feminine role-playing that the "normal" man-woman relationship requires. In a way, says de Beauvoir, "all women are naturally homosexual."

Commentary

This is the first time that de Beauvoir accords a woman free choice. Until now all her women have been extremely passive and servile. But it takes a lesbian, someone who rejects family life and the traditional role of woman, to be able to exercise this free will, or as de Beauvoir calls it, "masculine freedom."

As for homosexuality, de Beauvoir's liberal views are much ahead of her time. She rejects any moral indignation. For her, homosexuality is not perversion or a curse but largely a matter of free choice. Choosing to be a lesbian is one way for a woman to solve the unacceptable role of passive woman that society demands of her.

De Beauvoir's dealing with a subject long taboo attests to her intellectual honesty and verbal bravery. In 1976, close to 30 years after the publication of *The Second Sex*, de Beauvoir was interviewed by Alice Schwarzer, a German journalist and feminist. She elaborated on her ideas of lesbianism: "In itself, female homosexuality is just as restricting as heterosexuality." But, she added, "the ideal thing would be to be able to love a woman just as well as a man, a human being pure and simple, without fear, without pressure, without obligations." When interviewed again by Alice Schwarzer in 1982, de Beauvoir said, in answer to a question about her own experience with homosexuality, that although she had close friendships with women, they never aroused erotic passion in her, most probably because of her traditional education. "Women should not let themselves be conditioned exclusively to male desire any more. And in any case, I think that these days every woman is a bit ... a bit homosexual."

This chapter ends Part IV of *The Second Sex*, dedicated to the female formative years - the woman as a young girl and an adolescent, experiencing sexual awakening and first sexual activity, ending with the female homosexual who chooses to be free as lesbian rather than servile as wife. In Part V de Beauvoir will explore the situation of woman as an adult.

PART V: SITUATION

Chapter XVI: The Married Woman

The Argument

In marriage, the two sexes have never been on equal footing; man has always enjoyed economic and social independence while woman has been dependent on marriage for her support and justification, expected to satisfy male's sexual needs and provide society with children. While man focuses on projects outside the home, the home is the center of woman's life. She is doomed by marriage to repetition and routine.

Commentary

With insight and precision, de Beauvoir analyzes the condition of marriage for woman and for man as no one has done before her, upsetting centuries-old accepted ways of life. Aggressively, even vehemently, she denounces traditional marriage, showing the role of the wife and housewife as extremely demeaning and damaging for woman. There is "no symmetry" in the situation of man and woman within marriage, which is but "a relic of dead ways of life." The husband is always the productive and creative party who contributes to the building of society, while woman is doomed to the boring, repetitious, unrewarding, and uncreative housework. De Beauvoir's negative attitude toward housework is often quoted and could scarcely be expressed in stronger terms:

> **Few tasks are more like the torture of Sisyphus than housework, with its endless repetition.... Washing, ironing, sweeping, ferreting out rolls of lint from under wardrobes - all this halting of decay is also the**

denial of life; for time simultaneously creates and destroys, and only its negative aspect concerns the housekeeper.

Nothing the housewife does has durable meaning. De Beauvoir angrily follows the young wife from her first hesitations and sexual innocence to becoming an all-controlling, bitter, frustrated, and jealous matron. She lashes out at the wife whose home is the sole center of her life, and admires the husband who looks for self-expression outside the home.

Here de Beauvoir does not blame the husband for the degradation and the futile role of woman as wife and housewife, but she perceives the failure of marriages as rooted in the very institution of marriage. For her, marriage and love are not synonymous: while marriage is duty, love is spontaneous, and only "divine intervention" will reconcile the two.

Ending the chapter on a hopeful note, de Beauvoir offers a scenario for a different relationship between man and woman: "a union freely entered upon by the consent of two independent persons," similar to contracting partners. This will come about only when both man and woman will be independent and fulfilled, each absorbed in his own work.

Today we are beginning to witness more of this kind of union between two equal human beings, who are economically and psychologically independent, endowing the man-woman relationship with new meaning and vitality. There is no doubt that de Beauvoir's *The Second Sex* as well as the example of her independent lifestyle have greatly contributed to this progress.

CHAPTER XVII: THE MOTHER

The Argument

Pregnancy and motherhood, de Beauvoir says, are detrimental to woman. Pregnancy causes discomfort and deforms woman's body. Motherhood deprives woman of her freedom and prevents her from developing herself and having masculine careers.

Commentary

Of all the 25 chapters of *The Second Sex* none has provoked so much fury and indignation as Simone de Beauvoir's chapter on motherhood. Ordinary readers as well as devoted feminists who have endorsed many of her revolutionary ideas have rejected vehemently de Beauvoir's attitude toward motherhood. In fact, her refusal to see the significance of motherhood in woman's life is the biggest flaw in her theories of woman and it has prevented many feminists and admirers from endorsing her theories in full.

De Beauvoir writes about pregnancy with the same inexplicable disgust as she writes about the female body. For her, pregnancy is "injury," the fetus is "a parasite that feeds on" a woman's body, an "opulence [that] annihilates her," and makes her feel "that she is no longer anything," that she is merely "tossed and driven, the plaything of obscure forces," her body, "deformed" and "disfigured," turns upon itself "in nausea and discomfort," turning her into "a stock-pile of colloids, an incubator, an egg."

It is amazing how de Beauvoir, who has analyzed the condition of woman as girl and wife with so much insight and understanding, has failed completely in her study of the pregnant woman and mother. Has de Beauvoir, who had chosen not to bear children herself, expressed in this chapter her personal loathing of pregnancy and child-raising? Most pregnant women and mothers will not identify with her hostile and repugnant description of a condition that many women perceive as exhilarating and very fulfilling. Here de Beauvoir displays not only insensitivity, but also complete ignorance of the feeling of pregnant women and mothers, using abstract arguments to deny the existence of natural feeling. She may have based her conclusions on past centuries when women were subjected to an uninterrupted sequence of pregnancies and may have experienced the kind of sheer misery that de Beauvoir refers to.

Motherhood As Free Choice

In de Beauvoir's relentless and passionate battle to free woman from all barriers that may prevent her from fulfilling all her potential as a human being (including aspiring to positions of great power and prestige) she knocks down everything that may impede woman on her way to achieving them. Time and again de Beauvoir emphasizes the fact that maternity deprives woman of equal footing with man, that woman, enclosed in the home, "cannot establish her existence: she lacks the means requisite for self-affirmation as an individual." Glorification of motherhood as woman's sole destiny leaves woman little choice. What de Beauvoir is trying to say in her extreme way is that motherhood should be a matter of free choice, that a woman's sole destiny in life is not - as many advocate - to give birth and raise children, but that woman's destiny, like man's, is to live up to her potential as a human being. However, being a housewife and a mother has not always been chosen by woman but often been assigned to her, expected of her, and even imposed on her. Motherhood can be rewarding in favorable economic conditions if it is by choice, but this element of choice requires acceptance of contraception and abortion.

De Beauvoir never makes it completely clear whether she considers society or woman's biological makeup as responsible for woman's woes. Although in her first chapter she explicitly says that it is not woman's biology but society that is responsible for woman's inferior condition, this chapter on motherhood, which sees pregnancy as a deformity and the fetus as a parasite, clearly implies that woman's biological makeup is responsible for her situation.

Repetition: Bad And Good

Also strange and superficial is de Beauvoir's negative attitude toward repetition, placing it in opposition to creativity. On the superficial level, she may be right: repetition is boring. But on a deeper level repetition is the essence of life: the rising and setting of the sun, the cycle of day and night and of the seasons, the generations coming and going. These rhythms provide structure and predictability and satisfy deep needs of human nature. There is no life or nature without life repeating itself in endless variations.

Some of de Beauvoir's information is simply incorrect, such as her statement that "almost all spontaneous miscarriages are of psychic origin." The advancement of medicine has proved her wrong in many cases. Furthermore, inconsistencies abound in this chapter. At times we read of "the difficulty and grandeur of maternal love" and at others of the mother's "strange mixture of narcissism," her hopes "almost always dissatisfied," and of the "defenseless infants [who] are abandoned to her care."

The mother dominates her son and makes him really hers, forbidding "sport and playmates," but in a previous chapter, "Girls," de Beauvoir claims that while mothers curtail their daughters' freedom they respect that of their sons, who engage freely in sports and wrestling with playmates.

Nevertheless, if we ignore the inconsistencies, the gross overstatements, and the extremes of language, we will find important truths in de Beauvoir's attempt to refute some basic misconceptions: woman's destiny is solely to bear and raise children; motherhood is enough in all cases to fulfill a woman's life; mothers are always nurturing and supportive. De Beauvoir's unconventional point of view is an antidote to the traditional and often sentimental view that glorifies motherhood, elevating it to the status of sainthood.

Method At Fault

To prove her extreme ideas on motherhood, de Beauvoir quotes lavishly but selectively from Colette, Isadora Duncan, Colette Audry, and Leo Tolstoy as well as from different psychological studies. In no other chapter are the disadvantages and limitations of her research method so clear. Had she conducted a wide survey of women of all ages, classes, and races instead of searching the library for material supporting her preconceived ideas, she might have reached different conclusions.

During the years that followed the publication of *The Second Sex*, de Beauvoir tried to soften her harsh criticism of motherhood. She has admitted that under favorable conditions, such as adequate child-care, economic independence, and adequate domestic help, some women might even enjoy having children. But at the same time she has reiterated her objection to the prevalent view "which expects every woman to have children," stressing that "women are exploited - and they allow themselves to be exploited - in the name of love."

CHAPTER XVIII: SOCIAL LIFE

The Argument

Having no professional occupation except the home, woman concentrates on herself. Clothes, jewelry, and makeup serve as "uniform and an adornment," placing her body on display, a "prey to male desires." Social custom encourages her to "identify herself with her appearance," to turn herself into an "erotic object," while for man his clothes and appearance are not "a reflection of his ego."

Commentary

With sensitivity for nuances, de Beauvoir excels in analyzing women's attitude to clothes, makeup, and fashion, delineating women's obsession with their appearance as if it were the reflection of their egos. Women turn themselves into "a prop," "an object" meant to be "on view," in order to be seductive and attractive in men's eyes.

Considering de Beauvoir's generally negative attitude toward woman, it is surprising that she describes female friendship in such a positive light. Female friendship allows woman the only chance "to shake off her chains" and assert herself, to question male domination and male codes, to reject them and create her own values. However, de Beauvoir cannot conceal her general derogative view of woman and her admiration of man: while women always talk only about themselves and their feminine lot, it is men who discuss ideas and projects. Even woman's friendship as well as her love affairs and social life are but false escapes from the basic dismal condition of woman.

De Beauvoir's final conclusion, that man and woman can enjoy other lovers yet have a close relationship with each other, provided they have drawn up an agreement based on liberty and sincerity, is a general description of her own lifelong relationship with Sartre, a relationship that may or may not be suitable for other people.

CHAPTER XIX: PROSTITUTES AND HETAERAS

The Argument

There is little difference between a wife and a prostitute for both have sold themselves - the wife in marriage, the prostitute for money, and "for both the sexual act is a service." The only difference is that the wife is respected and has some rights, while the prostitute has no rights as a person and thus she "sums up all the forms of feminine slavery at once." But paradoxically, the high-class prostitute (the hetaera or the courtesan) has gained economic independence and enjoyed more freedom than any other woman of her times.

Commentary

It is ironic that the only woman whom de Beauvoir looks upon with generosity and even appreciation are those who live on the fringe of society - the lesbians and the courtesans. According to de Beauvoir, it is not the "respectable" women, but the unrespectable ones who have managed to escape the feminine destiny and have attained economic and mental freedom, living, in a way, like men. It is a pessimistic message: in the present day, the only way for woman to be free and live like man is to live outside respectability and marriage, in the margin of society, namely, to be a lesbian or a high-class prostitute.

De Beauvoir differentiates between two kinds of prostitutes: the high-class one who has won freedom and lives like a man, and the low-class one, who in her extreme poverty and misery symbolizes for de Beauvoir the general state of woman's slavery.

She draws an ironic parallel between high-class prostitutes and movie stars, whom she considers to be the modern representation of the courtesans. The movie star "yields woman over to the dreams of men, who repay her with wealth and fame." She depends solely on her producer to decide the color of her hair, her weight, and her figure; and she depends on her body, which ages.

"Marriage: The Greatest Trap"

Although the condition of woman has much improved since de Beauvoir wrote this chapter, she continued to believe, even to her final years, that the only way for a woman today to live free and independent is outside marriage and motherhood. Even though de Beauvoir did not go as far as to advise women to be hetaeras, she honestly believed that the only freedom possible for woman was to be single, live alone, and hold a job, just the way she herself lived all her life. In an interview in 1976 she said, "I think a woman should be on her guard against the trap of motherhood and marriage .... because marriage is really the biggest trap of all."

This chapter demonstrates de Beauvoir's remarkable ability to analyze a social condition and show it from a new perspective. To prove that a prostitute is not worse - in fact, is even more honest - than a legal wife, requires both courage and intellectual skill, of which de Beauvoir has plenty. Furthermore, this chapter is somewhat more concise and tightly written than the rest of the book. It teems with insightful and quotable sentences.

CHAPTER XX: FROM MATURITY TO OLD AGE

The Argument

Like menstruation, pregnancy, and childbirth, menopause is a crisis: suddenly woman is deprived of her femininity while half of her adult life is still ahead of her. Some women try to fight aging by pretending they are still young. But the crisis continues until woman accepts her growing old. Then, free of all her responsibilities, she can finally be a whole person.

Commentary

As de Beauvoir has no sympathy for the contemporary woman who accepts her secondary servile role in society, so she has no sympathy for the manner in which the contemporary woman grows old. De Beauvoir is angry at the aging woman just as she has been angry with the younger version. When they were young these women concentrated on their appearance, and now, suffering "mutilation," they are devastated. Just as they did nothing creative or useful for themselves or others when they were younger, they do nothing meaningful now, This is a great pity because it is the first time that woman is completely free to pursue her own interests.

De Beauvoir only insinuates, but does not elaborate in her usual detailed manner, the possibility that the older woman may finally begin a new chapter in her life as a human being. De Beauvoir is more interested in analyzing the present reality and making women aware of their situation than in offering concrete guidance or drawing up scenarios for the future. Nevertheless, her scant suggestion mounts to prediction, for in the eighties we have witnessed a phenomenon far greater than de Beauvoir could have ever foreseen: a fast-growing number of older women going back to school, finding employment, opening businesses and actually beginning their lives at retirement age, when their husbands, weary of years of working outside the home, are getting ready to retire to Florida.

CHAPTER XXI: WOMAN'S SITUATION AND CHARACTER

The Argument

Woman lacks "masculine logic" because, having been taught to accept masculine authority without questioning, she has never had the chance to use it. Since woman's life is made of repetitions, time for her means only deterioration - of body, of clothes, of furniture. Struggling against this deterioration, woman has become profoundly traditional, trying to conserve rather than to destroy and build anew, to compromise rather than to revolt. But her hope for liberation, as for all the oppressed, lies only in revolt: to achieve economic independence and collective power.

Commentary

Although much of this chapter has been previously stated, this is the first time that de Beauvoir offers a possible way out from woman's servile situation: revolution. The first step in this revolt is for woman to attain economic independence. The second step is collective female power, which will work toward the full emancipation of women.

While de Beauvoir has often discussed women getting jobs and being economically independent, this is the first time that she mentions the need for women's collective power. She does not elaborate, perhaps because when she wrote *The Second Sex*, the women's movement was inactive and did not assert itself fully until almost 20 years after publication of the book.

De Beauvoir, who is so indignant about woman's submissive condition, sees everything feminine as negative and everything masculine as positive. She hails "masculine logic" as the desired goal, as if "masculine logic" can bring an end to woman's woes. Today we know that not only man but woman, too, can use logic, and that logic alone does not provide all the answers; like emotions or instincts, it can develop in devious ways.

Contradiction

"A free individual blames only himself for his failures, he assumes responsibility for them," writes de Beauvoir. While this may be in line with her existentialist philosophy, it contradicts her main concept in *The Second Sex*: that man has made woman subordinate to him. If, according to the existentialist philosophy, every person is responsible for his failures, woman must be responsible for hers, and she, too, must take the blame for her secondary place in society. At the same time this concept returns to woman her dignity as a free human being who is responsible for her actions, something de Beauvoir has never accorded her. De Beauvoir has apparently sensed this discrepancy and has tried to reconcile her existentialist philosophy and her view of woman as victim. She writes: "But everything happens to woman through the agency of others, and therefore these others are responsible for her woes." This means that everyone, except woman, is responsible for himself, i.e., all men are responsible, and all women are not. This attitude, unfortunately, corresponds with the traditional derogatory male's view of woman.

In view of this discrepancy, one wonders: (1) what a study of woman's situation would be like if it were written from the existentialist point of view, meaning that woman, just like man, is responsible for her life and for her failures; and (2) whether *The Second Sex* corresponds more with de Beauvoir's personal, even emotional, biased outlook of woman than with an objective analysis.

On the hopeful note of woman's revolt and collective power, de Beauvoir ends the fifth part of her book, which has concentrated on the contemporary woman.

PART VI: JUSTIFICATIONS

Chapter XXII: The Narcissist

The Argument

De Beauvoir accepts the popular notion that "narcissism is the fundamental attitude of all women" and provides three reasons for this situation: (1) Woman feels frustrated because as a girl she lacked the boy's alter ego. (2) Woman is sexually unsatisfied. (3) Woman is denied masculine activities. "She is occupied, but she does nothing." Woman makes herself important because she has nothing important to do.

Commentary

De Beauvoir's argument in this chapter is questionable: she states a popular prejudice that women are narcissists, and then proceeds to explain why it is so, as if it were a fact. De Beauvoir is so skilled with words that one has the feeling that she can explain anything she chooses to explain.

Woman "does nothing" and therefore she is "nothing." Man is important because he does: "the houses he builds, the forests he clears, the maladies he cures." This differentiation between doing and being, with doing getting all the credit and being all the discredit, is surprising, coming from a philosopher and an intellectual. Does it mean that a person's morality and value system do not count? That what a person is and what he is not is meaningless? That it is time to change "to be or not to be" to "to do or not to do"? Coming from a thinker who, to a large extent, has gained her reputation by what she is and by the way she has chosen to be, this analysis is amazing if not absurd. Sometimes one has the feeling, at least in this chapter, that de Beauvoir has been carried away by her own rhetoric.

This chapter is replete with sentences (though often beautifully phrased) that suggest their opposite: "Women more than men cling to childhood memories." The opposite, that men cling to memories more than women, seems just as plausible. Likewise, couldn't her judgment about an actress: "third rater … concerned not for what she is accomplishing but for the glory it reflects on her; she thinks first of all to emphasize her own importance," just as easily be made of actors, too? For that matter, isn't it true for a great number of people in all professions, and maybe truer of the doers more than of the be-ers?

Indeed, the main idea of this chapter suggests its opposite: isn't narcissism a prevalent human characteristic, to be found in many men as well as women?

CHAPTER XXIII: THE WOMAN IN LOVE

The Argument

Love has a completely different meaning for man and for woman, according to de Beauvoir. For woman, love is her whole existence; she relinquishes everything for a lover and is "nonexistent without a master." For man, love is only "one value among others."

Accustomed to seeing the male as superior, woman turns her relationship with him into a religion, losing herself to man, body and soul. Most women keep dreaming of ideal love although reality has presented them only with imperfect substitutes.

Refusing to be an adult and take responsibility for her life, woman needs man for her security and maintenance. She has to feel that she is necessary and her existence justified.

Commentary

With subtlety and keen psychological understanding of women in love, de Beauvoir analyzes the entire gamut of romantic attachment: passion, expectations, possessiveness, jealousy, frustration, disappointment, and waiting. She rightly argues that woman, prevented from taking part in the action of the world, identifies so completely with her man and his project that she abdicates her identity and self, literally becoming he, and then calling this effacing of her personality "love." Moreover, in her relentless pursuit of ideal love, woman crushes her lover with her heavy expectations. This kind of love-master-slave is doomed to failure.

De Beauvoir's psychological analysis of woman's obsessive love seems true only for some women, those who, in the jargon of the eighties, are labeled "women who love too much," evoking Robin Norwood's book of the same title.

When de Beauvoir speaks about women who keep dreaming of ideal love, she is certainly right, but the question is: Don't men also dream of ideal love? As noted before, it seems that de Beauvoir's observation is true not specifically of women but of human nature in general.

True Love

After harshly criticizing the woman in love, showing that a woman who loves too much does not really know what true love is, de Beauvoir offers a fascinating and original treatise on her own understanding of true love, a treatise than can be easily embraced by contemporary, sophisticated, liberated women and men.

True love, says de Beauvoir, takes into consideration the human limitations of the lover. It is not "a mode of salvation, but a human interrelation." It is false to endow another human being with an absolute value. Denying man human weaknesses, woman crushes him with the burden of her expectations; then she is bitterly disappointed when he does not live up to her image of him. Her tyranny makes him a prisoner. (This observation is just as true of man's unrealistic expectations of woman.) The lover's absence is always torture to a woman. This kind of love is doomed: "Two lovers destined solely for each other are already dead: they die of ennui, of the slow agony of a love that feeds on itself."

"Genuine love ought to be founded on the mutual recognition of two liberties ... Love would be revelation of self by the gift of self." It would happen only if woman exists "essentially" like man, meaning, being economically independent and having a goal aside from man. Only then will "love in equality" be possible:

On the day when it will be possible for woman to love not in her weakness but in her strength, not to escape herself but to find herself, not to abase herself but to assert herself - on that day love will become for her, as for man, a source of life and not of mortal danger.

CHAPTER XXIV: THE MYSTIC

The Argument

When woman is denied human love, she may direct her adoration at God Himself. Although man may also burn with religious passion, his is more intellectual and purified; moreover, those woman outnumber men by far because "woman is habituated to living on her knees," expecting salvation to come from heaven, "where the males sit enthroned."

Commentary

This chapter ends Part VI of *The Second Sex*. In this part, called "Justifications," de Beauvoir claims that woman, finding no meaning in her life, needs justification for her existence, and she finds it in three main avenues: narcissism, love, and mysticism. Having no life of her own and no way to express herself, woman seeks fulfillment by doting on herself, on man, and if these fail to satisfy her, on God.

Having analyzed female narcissism and love as vicarious ways for woman to endow her life with content, de Beauvoir analyzes woman's devotion to religion. Here, too, woman's effort to endow her life with meaning fails. Religion, just as narcissism or love, only traps woman in an impotent situation: she is unable to assert her liberty and independence.

Once again de Beauvoir uses her talent for **satire** and mocks the mystic woman: she often confuses God and man, seeking in divine love what the amoureuse seeks in that of man: "the exaltation of her narcissism." Woman develops either a relation with something as unreal as God, or an unreal relation with a real person. In either case, her freedom remains thwarted.

The only way out of the trap, says de Beauvoir, is for woman to direct her energy not to love of herself, not to love of man, and not to love of God, but to human society.

However, de Beauvoir's discussion of woman mystics is ambiguous and adds little to her analysis of the condition of woman. It only attests to her eagerness to cover every possible ground and answer every possible question.

PART VII: TOWARD LIBERATION

Chapter XXV: The Independent Woman

The Argument

Even an economically independent woman has not yet achieved a moral, social, and psychological equality with man: (1) The disadvantages of her conditioning as a girl act against her. (2) Maternity can paralyze her career. (3) Psychologically she faces a dilemma: she is a professional and an economically independent person yet, being judged by her "toilette," she feels the urge to live a traditionally female role. This dilemma will be solved only when man is ready to love "an equal instead of a slave."

Commentary

In this final chapter, de Beauvoir sums up much of what she has said throughout her book, that in a man-made world, it is economic independence that will bring about woman's emancipation. Then, for the first time, she discusses the complex situation of the already liberated professional woman who lives in the present male-dominated society, suffering a split personality and juggling herself as a passive woman and as a free human being. To her credit, de Beauvoir grants woman the right to sexual freedom and breaks the taboo against discussing ways to attain it.

In bold and direct language, de Beauvoir demands for woman the same sexual freedom enjoyed by man: the busy professional woman needs "agreeable sexual adventures." The problem is that when woman pursues free sex, she, unlike man, risks her reputation. The solutions de Beauvoir dares to offer woman are revolutionary: (1) To establish bordellos for women. (2) To pick up a man in the street, although this may be physically dangerous. (3) To keep and support a lover, although a woman must be wealthy to afford it.

But even if the liberated woman manages to overcome her dilemma and the resulting inner confusion, her conditioning as a girl - being expected to achieve less than boys - will always be against her. For woman to be really equal, de Beauvoir says, she would have to be raised exactly like boys. Here again we find de Beauvoir's biased and uncritical admiration of male's behavior and way of life. She does not suggest that boys and girls should be raised equally; after all, boys can benefit from female education - to be gentle and peace-loving, as girls can benefit from male's - to be aggressive and competitive.

De Beauvoir has often been criticized for her espousal of male characteristics and the male situation as the ideals toward which woman should aspire: "It will be through attaining the same situation as theirs [men's] that [woman] will find emancipation." But man's own situation leaves much to be desired, with men being driven or dominated by power, money, and ambition. Few have attained a degree of spiritual condition as human beings that women could be envious of. De Beauvoir would be happy if women were like men, instead of advocating feminine qualities such as non-aggression, nurturing, gentility, kindness, peacefulness, patience, and spontaneity. Only once when she said, "We admire in Colette a spontaneity that is not met with in any male writer," did de Beauvoir suggest that what women should aspire to is not to match men or be like them but to be free to be themselves, and more of themselves.

Nevertheless, de Beauvoir's final chapter is also her most optimistic one. For the first time she acknowledges that men, too, will have to change if women are to gain true liberation. And there is evidence, de Beauvoir says, that men are beginning to change and adjust themselves to the new woman. True love and meaningful relationships are possible only if both parties are free, independent and assertive human beings and mutually respectful of each other. De Beauvoir implies, but stops short of saying explicitly, that for women to gain liberation men will have to be liberated too.

Once again de Beauvoir returns to the question that has long been troubling her: Why are there no women geniuses? This time her answer is that women were denied access to the world and to human experiences outside the home - the necessary conditions for geniuses to flourish. Women were denied the Belgian coal mines, the solitude of Arles, the cafes and brothels that constituted Van Gogh's experience. (But if this is so, one wonders, how can the poetry of Emily Dickinson, who never left her home, be explained?)

According to de Beauvoir, even the handful of women who have "made it" in a male's world have not achieved the greatness of the male writers because women writers have been too timid "to emerge beyond the given world," and thus unable to undertake daring flights. However, some have challenged society and created a powerful "literature of protest":

> **Virginia Woolf has made us see (that) Jane Austen, the Bronte sisters, George Eliot, have had to expend so much energy negatively in order to free themselves from outward restraints that they arrive somewhat out of breath at the stage from which masculine writers of great scope take their departure.**

This is why, though splendid, *Middlemarch* is not equal to *War and Peace*, or *Wuthering Heights* to *The Brothers Karamazov*. Although today it is easier for women to assert themselves, contemporary female writers are still too busy seeing the facts and understanding reality to venture beyond these and discover meanings and a "secret dimension." They sometimes excel in the observation of facts, and thus make remarkable reporters. As writers they concentrate on description of atmosphere and characters as well as of nature. But no woman has written a *Moby Dick* or a *Ulysses*. "Women do not contest the human situation, because they have hardly begun to assume it." They take the world as it is too seriously without asking fundamental questions.

Great men have all assumed the enormous burden of the world upon their shoulders, something no woman has ever done nor could have. "To regard the universe as one's own, to consider oneself to blame for its faults and to glory in its progress, one must belong to the caste of the privileged." Except for St. Theresa, there is hardly a woman who lived out the situation of humanity in total abandonment as did Van Gogh or Kafka, for instance. As long as a woman "still has to struggle to become a human being, she cannot become a creator." Some people claim that women lack "creative genius." But "how could women ever have had genius when they were denied all possibility of accomplishing a work of genius - or just a work?"

De Beauvoir's manner of grading writers and artists and pitting them against each other as if they were all in the same arena, racing to the finish line, is disconcerting. Whether Tolstoy is greater than George Eliot, *The Brothers Karamazov* better than *Wuthering Heights*, is irrelevant, because Tolstoy and Jane Austen, Feodor Dostoyevsky and Emily Bronte, with all their differences, are equally an integral part of our human culture and experience.

The final chapter of *The Second Sex* ends with a positive declaration: "The free woman is just being born." It is high time that she take her chances "in her own interest and in the interest of all."

Stylistically, this is one of the better organized and more densely written chapters, leading the readers from one argument to another without losing them in the process.

CONCLUSION

The Argument

Men and women, says de Beauvoir in the conclusion of her book, are not friends and are unsatisfied with each other. The main question is whether this stage is natural or only transitional. Analyzing both possibilities, de Beauvoir concludes that the present hostility between the sexes does not stem from physiological or natural factors but is the direct result of female oppression, since "all oppression creates a state of war." This conflict will continue until men and women recognize each other as peers and equals.

Commentary

This is a most fitting ending to this massive book: a "prayer" for men and women to be brothers. But it is regrettable that even her very last word is taken from the male world: brotherhood (fraternité). Not sisterhood, or even a gender-free word such as solidarity is used to describe the ultimate relationship between men and women. Nevertheless, she does envision a better and happier state awaiting the sexes sometime in the future, a state of mutual respect and recognition of the other as peer, when love and passion will assume their original meaning. No longer will enslavement and hypocrisy dominate relationships, but a true and honest need for each other will be exercised in freedom to the full advantage of both men and women.

Lack Of Tactics For Emancipation

One of the strongest criticisms of *The Second Sex* has come from feminists, who have claimed that de Beauvoir, who so brilliantly analyzed the inferior situation of woman in society, has stopped short of suggesting ways for women to change this situation and pursue freedom and independence. True, de Beauvoir has opened women's eyes and made them aware of their condition as never before, but what then? How can woman, still the second sex, achieve freedom? How can she break the tradition of centuries and become - psychologically and practically - liberated and independent? In short, women who read *The Second Sex* may become profoundly aware of their secondary role in a male-dominated society but will have no idea what to do about it.

De Beauvoir's first reaction to this criticism was that her task was to analyze woman's condition, but that each woman must find the right solution for herself. Only years later, in an interview with Alice Schwarzer, did de Beauvoir admit that the main shortcoming of her book is the lack of tactics for the emancipation of woman. Yet, in her long and pioneering essay, de Beauvoir does indicate sporadically the desired road for women to take. She has stressed the importance of having a job as the single most important step toward independence, the only way for a woman to have a life of her own. She does warn women against falling into the trap of housekeeping and motherhood as woman's only employment. And if a woman still wants a child she would do well to have one outside marriage since marriage, as it is practiced today, is the biggest trap of all.

But how can a wife and mother lacking a profession attain her liberation? For her, de Beauvoir offers no plan of action. In 1976 she told Alice Schwarzer that these women "really don't stand much of a chance. If they are thirty-five, with four children to cope with, married and lacking any professional qualifications - then I don't know what they can do to liberate themselves. You can only talk about the real prospect of liberation for future generations." Here, fortunately, de Beauvoir has erred. Since the awareness brought about by *The Second Sex*, followed later by the Women's Liberation Movement, women of all ages, even married women and senior citizens, have begun to pursue professional training, returning to college, and finding employment.

But on the whole, as de Beauvoir has written with such persuasion, much of woman's liberation depends on social change. Society as a whole, as well as men and women, has to change to allow both sexes equality and freedom; that means equal education for girls, the availability of contraception and abortion to make maternity voluntary, the liberation of women from housework, and appropriate day-care centers to allow women who have chosen motherhood to pursue their careers.

Although much improvement has taken place since the publication of *The Second Sex*, women and men are still in a state of war with each other and have a long way to go before they will become friends, comrades, and colleagues. But de Beauvoir is optimistic; she envisions the possibility of a creative and supportive relationship of man and woman as equals and as peers who are joined in marriage that is based on free agreement and dissoluble at will.

Here, for the first time, de Beauvoir acknowledges that equality between the sexes does not mean sameness. There will always be some differences between men and women. But once "the slavery of half of humanity" will be abolished, women and men will be able to "affirm their brotherhood." Her unshaking belief in the possibility of creating a better and more just society for women and men is uplifting.

It seems that Simone de Beauvoir's main departure from Sartre's existentialism is her unflagging, even contagious, optimism. Sartre's concept of the individual's total freedom has led him to profound nihilism. He maintained that anxiety and anguish underlie all human existence and thus rejected all ideas of happiness, well-being and optimism as superficial, naive, and stupid, the denial of the tragic aspect of human existence. De Beauvoir, on the other hand, has declared that she had never met anyone in the whole of her life who was so well equipped for happiness as she was, or who labored so hard to achieve it.

Although de Beauvoir adopted the main points of Sartre's existentialism, i.e., that the individual has freedom of choice and that he is responsible for his choices, she reached a different conclusion: one can also choose to be happy.

The Second Sex is an extremely optimistic book, overflowing with passion for life, and ending with a strong belief in the possibility of creating a better and happier society for men and women.

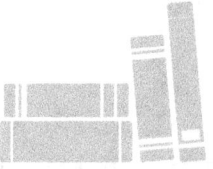

THE SECOND SEX

CRITICS RESPOND TO THE SECOND SEX

When *The Second Sex* first appeared in France in June 1949, it unleashed an unparalleled storm, evoking as much admiration as indignation. Some critics compared the book with such influential classics as John Stuart Mill's *On the Subjection of Women* (1869) and Mary Wollstonecraft's *A Vindication of the Rights of Women* (1792). Some even went so far as to compare it with Karl Marx's *Das Kapital* (1867), a work that changed the course of history. At the same time other critics made *The Second Sex* and its writer the target of violent outrage, insult, and even obscenity.

CAMUS INSULTED

In fact, the scandal burst into the open even before publication of the book, when the chapter "Woman's Sexual Initiation" appeared in *Les Temps Modernes* in May, followed by "The Lesbian" in June. Albert Camus, the influential writer and philosopher, perceived de Beauvoir's ideas as an affront to his masculinity, and in a fury accused her of ridiculing the French male. Even more indignant and vocal was the distinguished Catholic writer Francois Mauriac (who would win the Noble Prize for literature in 1952). Immediately he began a vicious crusade against the book. In the influential *Le Figaro Litteraire*, he wrote, "We have literally reached the limits of the abject. This is the ipecac they made us swallow as children to induce vomiting. Here perhaps is the moment of the final nausea: that which delivers" (June 25, 1949). To the staff of *Les Temps Modernes*, he wrote, "I've learned all there is to know about your boss's vagina." Mauriac's obscene reaction evoked the fury of the critic Domenach who, in the left-wing Christian review Esprit, hailed Simone de Beauvoir's courage in offering her readers "a course in normal sexuality," and suggested that novelists like Francois Mauriac were furious because de Beauvoir brought to light the subterranean sources of sexuality from which those novelists drew their themes.

In answer to Domenach, Andre Rousseau offered a sarcastic and condescending view of *The Second Sex* in *Le Figaro Litteraire* (November 12, 1949):

> ...In raising my eyes from Mme. de Beauvoir's book I look around me in search of the dens of females and the harems, the herds of female slaves whose lives, because of masculine imperialism, might be divided up between servile tasks and male pleasure ... our Amazon, in stirring up one half of humanity in revolt against the other, is comparable only to the world's great revolutions ... I have very little faith in the future of this revolution based on pedantry and bedroom. This attempt to destroy woman by a woman of letters left me afflicted more by lassitude than disgust.

Instead of reasonably and professionally arguing with de Beauvoir's ideas, the critics' violent reaction displayed an emotional attack against the writer, a behavior unbefitting men of culture. Apparently, de Beauvoir had touched a very sensitive and profound nerve in the life of these critics, and each felt as if she had attacked him personally. She dared to question the sacredness of many taboos that had been the basis of Western religion and culture for centuries, namely the validity of the family as it had been run and structured, the fairness of the division of labor in the family, woman's role and status as wife, mother, and human being.

"FIRST WOMAN PHILOSOPHER"

On the other extreme was *Paris Match*. In a seven-page article (August 6, 1949) it hailed Simone de Beauvoir as "the first woman philosopher to appear in the history of man," a woman who "explodes cliches" and "summons women to freedom a woman who "extracts from the grand human adventure a philosophy of her sex." And a writer who deals with:

> **all the problems that characterize the modern woman's restlessness and worry: the freedom to live, abortion, prostitution, sexual equality, marriage and divorce, giving birth painlessly, etc. ... Biology alone won't yield an answer. It's a matter of knowing what humanity has made of the human female.**

In February 1953, *The Second Sex* was published in the United States, translated, edited, and somewhat abbreviated by H. M. Parshley. It was an immediate success. The American critics, just like their French colleagues, took extreme positions, though their tone was much milder. After all, the general status of women in America at that time was more progressive than in France. In 1920, American women gained voting rights nationally, a quarter of a century before they did in France, but already in 1869 they had won the right to vote in Wyoming. Moreover, American woman had easier access to contraception and abortion on the one hand, and to education and career on the other. "Anyway," said de Beauvoir, "it's easier to tolerate a foreigner..."

"IT TOOK A WOMAN TO DO IT"

Ashley Montagu, a writer and the chairman of the anthropology department at Rutgers University, wrote in the *New York Herald Tribune Book Review* (February 22, 1953) that *The Second Sex* is "one of the great expressions of the human spirit of our culture. [It is] the healthiest, headiest, wealthiest, and wisest book that has ever been written on women and, therefore, also on men. It will be read, I predict, for generations." And in *The Saturday Review* (February 21, 1953) the same reviewer suggests to every woman in doubt to read the book that will free her from the tyranny of manmade myths about the inferiority of women. This great book, he continued, is noted for:

> **its qualities of analysis, restraint, eloquence, and the influence it is bound to have upon human thought and conduct.... The book is beautifully written in all senses of the word.... While the book could have been written by a man, it took a woman to do it.**

Of the same admiring opinion was Clyde Kluckhohn, professor of anthropology at Harvard, who wrote in the *New York Times* (February 22, 1953) that this is "literature in the grand sense. I cannot think of a single American scholar, man or woman, who controls such a vast body of knowledge as this

French writer. In spite of its immense learning, this is never a dull book." He admired the book for its "beautiful language and imagery," and of the chapter, "The Myth of Woman in Five Authors," he remarked that it is "so well done that one gets the same kind of almost physical pleasure that one does from the superb performance of music that matters."

However, Kluckhohn voiced some interesting reservations. He thought that Simone de Beauvoir:

> **underestimates the extent to which women can be creative and "free" through the exercise of household responsibilities which need not be nearly as demeaning or "enslaving" as filing the same kinds of papers day by day or repeating endlessly the same routines in a factory. If one presses some of the author's statements to their logical extremes, it would seem that she wanted and thought it possible that all women should become artists or intellectuals. We know that neither all men nor all women have such potentialities.**

"TRULY MAGNIFICENT BOOK"

In other words, Kluckhohn says that de Beauvoir greatly exaggerates when she considers household work to be so dehumanizing and enslaving to women, and certainly it is not more so than the dull and repetitive work at the office or factory. Secondly, even if women were to be free of household responsibilities, most of them would not become artists or intellectuals, as de Beauvoir assumes they would, because most people, men or women, do not possess such talents. In addition, Kluckhohn thinks that the book says too much about sexuality and "relatively little [is] said [though well] about economic, political, and social factors." However, his adverse criticism pales against his admiration of this "truly magnificent book even if sometimes irritating to a mere male."

The general chorus of adulation is joined by Bernard Gill of the *New Yorker* (February 23, 1953):

> ... more than a work of scholarship; it is a work of art, with the salt of recklessness that makes art sting ... she is not only getting rid of Eve and other images of woman as a mere afterthought of man, she is calling out with Whitman, "O to have life henceforth a poem of new joys!" This is her poem, her beautiful and sometimes blundering "Leaves of Grass" ... her statement of what men can be and women have never been allowed to be is a noble one.

A more critical approach is adopted by Patrick Mullahy, a professor of philosophy and psychoanalytical theory. *Writing in The Nation* of February 21, 1953, he agrees that it is a superb book brilliantly written with keen psychological insight; nevertheless, one has to read it with critical caution because of Mme. de Beauvoir's political leanings. What he means is that de Beauvoir's leftist inclination may have colored her study of woman's status. Unfortunately, he does not elaborate on this point.

Mullahy does present a poignant question: "Why do women not fundamentally challenge male sovereignty? How [does one] explain the submission of women?" After all, other oppressed groups liberate themselves in one way or another. Why does woman not free herself from man, her oppressor? *The Second Sex*, he says, attempts to answer this question by explaining that the bond uniting woman and man is unlike any other. But although man and woman constitute a basic unity, woman is not equal but the "Other" in this unity. Then Mullahy criticizes de Beauvoir for not offering "concrete counsel as to how both men and women can solve their problems." De Beauvoir, he comments, is a bit naive and not facing the "enormous complexities that any advanced society has to deal with." Being a romantic individualist, she does not realize that:

> **woman's problems are part of a wider problem of interpersonal relations in family, school, workplace, community, and society in general. To understand this we need a more powerful psychology than Mme. de Beauvoir possesses and a more powerful sociology and social philosophy. She has done an excellent job ... But her suggestions are too simple to be of much use in working out a solution to woman's problems.**

In spite of his reservations, Mullahy considers the book a first-rate individual achievement and a delight to read. It will, no doubt, help to dispel many of the habitual notions and prejudices about women.

MEAD FINDS FLAWS

An intriguing concept was adopted by *The Saturday Review*. Its editors assigned the review of *The Second Sex* to five professionals and a housewife. Here we have the first review by a woman professional, the noted anthropologist Margaret Mead. She, too, agrees that the book provides a "rare, exasperating, but unfailingly interesting experience. It is torrential, brilliant, wonderfully angry." However, in spite of its brilliance, it violates every canon of science and disinterested scholarship in its partisan selectivity. Margaret Mead finds two main flaws: The first is a personal bias that expresses "the psychology of one woman whose society has convinced her that it is terrible to be born a woman." And the second flaw is the author's adamant refusal to recognize anything creative in maternity. De Beauvoir "constructs a picture in which the only way a woman can be a full human being is to be as much like a man as possible."

Margaret Mead's objections - that in *The Second Sex* de Beauvoir expresses a personal opinion rather than a scientific truth, that she denies the creativity and joys of maternity, that she denigrates feminine qualities and hails masculine ones - will be shared by many of de Beauvoir's critics and readers.

The second critic of *The Saturday Review*, the novelist and short-story writer Philip Wylie, had only praise. "One of the few great books of our era," he writes. Every person who wishes to be considered contemporary or intellectual cannot miss reading it, the same way he cannot miss reading Freud or Einstein or Darwin. The book, he claims:

> **flows from a quality men often deny to women: genius - at least by my definition of that lofty capacity. Genius, I think, is the ability to discover or to create a new category or a new dimension of human knowledge, human understanding, or human experience. Simone de Beauvoir has finally succeeded in adding that much insight to the subject of Woman and the twice-larger subject of human sexuality ...**

Wylie goes out of his way to praise de Beauvoir's achievement and her contribution to human awareness, her erudition, scholarly patience, and "cerebral appetite." This is the "reverence of a male," he reminds the reader, and "one known as a leading and angry critic of women." By asking the right questions, he writes, de Beauvoir challenges us to look for answers. In contrast to Mullahy of *The Nation*, who faults the book for lack of any concrete suggestions, Wylie praises it for just that: evoking the right questions and challenging us for the answers.

MENNINGER: THUMBS DOWN

The third reviewer of *The Saturday Review*, the psychiatrist Karl A. Menninger, downgrades the book outright, finding nothing redeeming in it. Not only is this not a masterpiece, as the publisher "modestly refers to it," but, in fact, it is a "pretentious and inflated tract on feminism. Hence it is intrinsically tiresome and it is made more so by the author's compulsion to repeat each idea many times, often in almost the same words as well as in paraphrases …. It is not good scientific writing … it is cast in a pseudo-scientific mold and invokes all possible support from scientific data."

Although he admits that some readers may be charmed by the "graceful and even eloquent passages" that permeate the book, some will be "disquieted by the plaintive, mildly paranoid wails that dot almost every page." He continues with this patronizing and denigrating tone when he draws on his professional experience:

> Mlle. de Beauvoir's picture of an aggressive male cavalierly oppressing and abusing women in lustful glee is largely a fantasy. Every psychiatrist sees a dozen women complain of the passivity, dependence, and/or impotence of their husbands to one who

complains of his ruthlessness .... I doubt that French men and women differ very much from American men and women .... this is not to deny that women are frustrated, but so are men.

Although Menninger admits that de Beauvoir may be right in her factual details, he considers her interpretation of these data as another one of those "myths" on which she elaborates in her book.

A HOUSEWIFE'S VIEW

The Saturday Review chose Phyllis McGinley, a self-proclaimed housewife and a poet of "light verse," to represent the opinion of American housewives. Unfortunately, de Beauvoir's ideas were lost on this housewife, who claimed that it does not matter who writes the novels and paints the pictures. If the woman's role is "to hold the world together while things are created" she must be proud of her secondary role.

This immense book, McGinley writes, is "old-fashioned," and its so-called radical ideas "we espoused when we were seventeen," meaning apparently that women like herself were radical and freedom-seeking in their teens, but later, when they came to their senses, they renounced their rebellious ideas and settled for what society had to offer them. The **irony** is that Simone de Beauvoir wrote her book about housewives like Phyllis McGinley. Mockingly, McGinley says that although she always considered herself a rebel and emancipated woman, *The Second Sex* proved to her that she is a sad conformist, a slave, a dupe, a victim:

> **I now stand exposed as one member of the most oppressed minority group in human history,** ***the***

Second Sex. How blind I have been! Christian nations have persecuted the Jew. Anglo-Saxon countries have done badly by the Negro. But the whole race of men, for thousands of years and everywhere on the face of earth, have been engaged in one vast conspiracy to enslave his comrade, Woman.

"WITHOUT A PLAN"

This stupendous, preposterous book, she adds, is readable as a novel though twice as romantic. Simone de Beauvoir likes to overthrow religion and abolish marriage but she does not tell us how to do it. Condescendingly, she writes, "Mademoiselle is without a plan." Then McGinley becomes dead serious, and her **irony** changes to anger:

> **Millions of deluded women believe themselves ennobled by the mere fact of being women. They may deplore the death of domestic servants or the lack of some gadget owned by a luckier neighbor. They may even envy their husband's wage-earning excuse for reaching the television set first in the evening while they are still inserting the plates into the automatic dishwasher. But by and large, they have convinced themselves or been convinced by their overlords that they are the luckier sex ... The children of the race belong to them as never before in history. Who'd want to settle for simply being a man?**

This housewife, at least, seems to be not only happy in her role of housewife but also proud of it. No doubt that she represents a large segment of American women. On the other hand, to her very last day, Simone de Beauvoir kept receiving letters from women, mostly housewives, who thanked her for giving voice to their hidden feelings and frustrations and were grateful for the strength and courage with which her book had endowed them.

Another disappointed reviewer is M. A. deFord of the *San Francisco Chronicle* (February 22, 1953). On the whole, he writes:

> **... this is a disappointing and unsatisfactory book. The author has too many dogmas and theses to ride, which limit her too severely and prevent this from being the definitive summing - up of the whole question, which the translator's preface and the jacket-blurb promise. Fundamentally it is a mountain that labors mightily and produces a very small and shopworn mouse.**

Time has not diminished the interest in *The Second Sex*. Years after its publication, scholars have kept arguing with its ideas. Two interesting studies appeared in 1967, almost 20 years after its first appearance in France.

BEAUVOIR "BIASED"

The literary critic C. B. Radford admits that Simone de Beauvoir is "probably right about the male," though her views of man are as distorted as are male's views of woman. Questioning her methods of argumentation, he suggests that her feminism is biased by her "three other preoccupations - the existential, the autobiographical, and the political":

The vehemence and aggressive style and the extreme nature of many of her views show a personal flair and an outspokenness that are rare in any other feminist writer. In fact, far more than the theories, it is the personal flavour that is the distinctive element of her feminism.

Radford deplores de Beauvoir's narrow scope, noting her frequent mistake of discussing the middle-class Western Woman as if she were all women, and thus limiting the value of her book to the broad movement of feminism. (C. B. Radford, "Simone de Beauvoir: Feminism's Friend or Foe?," in *Nottingham French Studies*, October 1967, May 1968.)

The same year, 1967, Henry Peyre, a Sterling Professor of French at Yale University and the author of many books, grants Simone de Beauvoir the highest compliments in his book *French Novelists of Today* (1967):

No French woman writer as yet has probably risen to the stature of Jane Austen or of Virginia Woolf, of Willa Cather, perhaps even of Edith Wharton. The exception, towering above all other women writers, may well be Simone de Beauvoir.

"A RARE WISDOM"

She has achieved "the most formidable vindication of women's rights since Mary Wollstonecraft." In 1975 Henry Peyre restates his esteem in his introduction to Jean Leighton's *Simone de Beauvoir on Woman* (1975), calling her "a pioneer in shaking our prejudices," and her book "a rare wisdom." He is nevertheless not blind to some of her flaws: her hasty reasoning and lack of common sense, contradictions in her writing, her rejection of motherhood (which has alienated many liberated women), her harsh criticism of the inferiority of her sex as "incapable of self-criticism and lofty ambitions," her "excessive adulation of male creative activity," the fact that the information in her often "confused book" is drawn from a mass of second-hand material are all problematic elements noted by Peyre.

Since 1974, the 25th anniversary of *The Second Sex* (an occasion that spawned many conferences and numerous articles in France and abroad), seven books dedicated to the study of Simone de Beauvoir's writing and thoughts have been published in the USA alone.

In her book *Simone de Beauvoir on Woman*, Leighton expresses some of the criticism that would be voiced by many feminists, accusing de Beauvoir of being "a misogynist," a woman-hater, and her much admired *Second Sex* "a diatribe against the female sex." Leighton writes: "Perhaps *The Second Sex* would make cheerful reading for men, so insistent and unwavering is its overestimation of the male." He is such an enviable creature, strong, independent, creative, and energetic. At the same time de Beauvoir dwells on "the horror of dependence in women." She considers dependence, passivity, and weakness as moral flaws while she admires domination and virile strength. But "it is the equality between the sexes and not domination by the woman that feminists have always sought."

"MEN, TOO, SUFFER"

Anne Whitmarsh, in *Simone de Beauvoir and the Limits of Commitment* (1981), takes this attitude a step further and offers a very intriguing thought:

> ... many of those fighting for women's liberation are convinced that society would be better if the 'feminine' virtues were to be adopted as its values. Simone de Beauvoir's notion of a sexually egalitarian society appears to be one in which women are able to display the masculine characteristics of aggressiveness, competitiveness and action, leading to fame and power. She has refused to say that feminine qualities (gentleness, compassion, sensitivity) are better than masculine qualities... In the debates that have taken place over the last ten years it has emerged that men, too, suffer from the constraints imposed by their dominant role, which does not necessarily fulfill them.

In *Simon de Beauvoir: A Life of Freedom* (1981), Carol Ascher tries to explain de Beauvoir's extreme attitude toward the sexes - her denigration of women and adoration of men - by pointing out de Beauvoir's isolation from any movement or community of women while writing the book. Although Ascher greatly admires the writer and her book, she criticizes it for depicting a world where "radical feminism is the only solution: a world where there really is no possible accord between women and men." De Beauvoir has little love or patience with female biology and the female social role; she believes that "all those qualities that make women differ from men only lead to their demise." While her description of a male-dominated world would spur women to "band together and go off on their own," de Beauvoir's dislike of women, "a kind of self-hatred," makes this banding together unattractive. "It's a cul-de-sac that many women, including myself, have felt." In spite of her reservations, Ascher admits that the book is "a miracle of courage and creativity."

WOMEN'S POWER?

An interesting point was raised by Mary Lowenthal Felstiner on the occasion of the 30th anniversary of *The Second Sex*. What about women's power? *The Second Sex* tells us only half of what women want to know: "the ways male domination constrains women," but it does not tell us the other half: "the ways women's power sets the world moving." To prove her point, Felstiner reports of studies that have been done since the publication of *The Second Sex* (and no doubt instigated by it) that point to periods in history in which women served as the domineering force (*Feminist Studies* 6, No.2, Summer 1980).

The wealth of material, studies, books, and on-going debates inspired by *The Second Sex* continue to gather momentum. The effort to assess the effect of the book on generations of women, and not less so on generations of men, as well as on the relationship between the sexes, has apparently reached only its initial stages.

THE SECOND SEX

IDEAS FOR PAPERS, ORAL REPORTS, AND CLASS DISCUSSION

- In what way is *The Second Sex* regarded as the Bible of the women's liberation movement?

- Throughout history woman has played a secondary role, says de Beauvoir. What are the reasons she gives for woman's inferior situation? Discuss the reasons from the biological, the psychological, and the social aspects.

- When and in what circumstances did woman - according to de Beauvoir - become inferior to man?

- What characteristics have made woman an easy prey to man's domination? How can woman overcome her disadvantages in our contemporary society?

- Why have women never protested or rebelled against their male oppressors the way other oppressed people, like the Irish or the blacks, challenged theirs?

- In what way was the Industrial Revolution a turning point in woman's situation?

- Women make their choices not in accordance with their nature but with man's expectations of them, claims de Beauvoir. Society's view of woman is not what woman really is, but what man's image of her is, what the myth of woman he created for himself portrays. How does man see woman and how does woman comply with man's expectations?

- Even a liberated woman, claims de Beauvoir, has one great disadvantage with reference to man - her education as a girl. Explain how a girl's education differs from that of a boy, and how it influences her adult life. Is de Beauvoir's description of the female adolescent's education relevant to the education of girls in our present society?

- Discuss de Beauvoir's views on female biological makeup. How have her critics reacted to them?

- How does a young woman's first sexual experience differ from that of a young man, and why?

- Marriage is woman's biggest trap, declares de Beauvoir. Discuss her arguments and her solutions. Explain your own views based on your observation of married women.

- De Beauvoir's views of woman as mother infuriated many people, even devout feminists. Discuss the issue and then express your own views on the matter.

- Discuss the role contraceptives and abortion play in the emancipation of women, as de Beauvoir sees it.

- Authoritarian regimes as a rule deny women access to contraceptives and abortion, says de Beauvoir, although she does not elaborate. Can you explain why this may be so?

- Why is de Beauvoir so negative about the woman in love?

- Of all the women described by de Beauvoir, why have only the lesbians and the prostitutes won her respect?

- When woman is prevented from living as a full human being, she is forced to concentrate on externals such as her appearance and her social life. Discuss de Beauvoir's reasoning and then express your own opinion.

- On several occasions de Beauvoir mentions female Hollywood stars to illustrate her theories. In what way do they serve her purpose?

- Once her children have left home, what options are left to the older woman (according to de Beauvoir; according to you)?

- If a woman wants to live up to her potential and not be subservient to man, how should she conduct her life, according to de Beauvoir? What is de Beauvoir's idea of the true woman?

- The liberated, professional woman of today faces many disadvantages in comparison to man. Discuss de Beauvoir's analysis of the liberated woman and her options.

- De Beauvoir's very definite idea of what male qualities are vis-a-vis female qualities has enraged many modern feminists. Discuss de Beauvoir's views, the feminists' criticism of her views, and your own.

- De Beauvoir believes that man and woman can develop a different relationship with each other based on equality. How does she see this new relationship?

- One of the antifeminists' strongest arguments is the lack of a female Shakespeare or a female Dante. What is de Beauvoir's answer to them? Do you find her answer convincing? Explain your views.

- In what way does de Beauvoir's own life reflect her idea of how a modern liberated woman should live as expressed in *The Second Sex*?

- Discuss the ways de Beauvoir uses or abuses language, sentence structure, and choice of words to bring forth her ideas.

- What are the main objections of feminists to *The Second Sex*?

- De Beauvoir claims that from the start, American women have been more liberated and less oppressed than their European sisters. Bring more evidence from American history to argue for or against de Beauvoir's view.

- De Beauvoir published *The Second Sex* in 1949. Has anything she discussed changed since then? Compare de Beauvoir's description of the dire situation of woman then with her situation now.

- Interview your mother, grandmother, or other women in your family, and find out how being a woman has affected their lives. Compare their stories with de Beauvoir's description of woman's inferior condition in *The Second Sex*.

- Interview four young female classmates, preferably of different races and nationalities, and find out the effect of their being a woman on their lives. Compare their experiences with that of de Beauvoir's woman. Has anything changed in woman's upbringing since the publication of the book?

- Prepare a questionnaire of 15 questions concerning: (1) the condition of woman; (2) the woman-man relationship; (3) the role that each of the sexes plays, or should play, in marriage and in raising and educating the children. Distribute it to men and women who are less than 40 years old (meaning, they were born after the publication of *The Second Sex*); then use their answers to write your own "*The Second Sex* - Forty Years Later," and compare your findings with those of de Beauvoir.

- What developments have occurred since de Beauvoir wrote *The Second Sex* that would have led her to different conclusions? In other words, if she had written the book today, in what ways would the new book differ from the original?

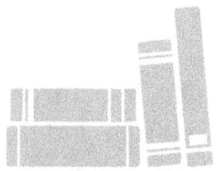

BIBLIOGRAPHY

EDITIONS OF SIMONE DE BEAUVOIR'S WORKS

Nonfiction

Pyrrhus et Cineas. Paris: Gallimard, 1944.

"Pyrrhus and Cineas." Selections, *Partisan Review*, III:3 (1946), pp. 430–437.

Pour une morale de l'ambiguite. Paris: Gallimard, 1947.

The Ethics of Ambiguity. New York: Philosophical Library, 1948.

L'Amerique au jour le jour. Paris: Mohrien, 1948.

America Day by Day. New York: Grove Press, 1953.

Le Deuxieme Sexe. Paris: Gallimard, 1949.

The Second Sex. New York: Knopf, 1953. New York: Vintage Books, 1974.

Privileges (essays). Paris: Gallimard, 1955.

Must We Burn Sade? New York: Grove Press, 1955.

La Longue Marche. Paris: Gallimard, 1957.

The Long March. Cleveland: World Publishing, 1958.

"Brigitte Bardot and the Lolita Syndrome" (article). *Esquire*, August 1959.

Brigitte Bardot and the Lolita Syndrome. New York: Arno Press and The New York Times, 1972.

"What Love Is - and Isn't" (article). *McCall's*, August 1967.

La Vieillesse. Paris: Gallimard, 1970.

The Coming of Age. New York: Putnam, 1972.

La Ceremonie des adieux. Paris: Gallimard, 1981.

Adieux: A Farewell to Sartre. New York: Pantheon, 1984.

Fiction

L'Invitee. Paris: Gallimard, 1943.

She Came to Stay. Cleveland: World Publishing, 1954.

Le Sang des autres. Paris: Gallimard, 1945.

The Blood of Others. New York: Knopf, 1948.

Tous les hommes sont mortels. Paris: Gallimard, 1946.

All Men Are Mortal. Cleveland: World Publishing, 1955.

Les Mandarins. Paris: Gallimard, 1954.

The Mandarins. Cleveland: World Publishing, 1956.

Les Belles Images. Paris: Gallimard, 1966.

Les Belles Images. New York: Putnam, 1968.

La Femme rompue (stories). Paris: Gallimard, 1966.

The Woman Destroyed. New York: Putnam, 1969.

Quand prime le spirituel (stories). Paris: Gallimard, 1980.

When Things of the Spirit Come First. New York: Pantheon, 1982.

Drama

Les Bouches inutiles. Paris: Gallimard, 1945.

Who Shall Die? Florissant, Missouri: River Press, 1983.

Memoirs

Memoires d'une jeune fille rangée (1908–1929). Paris: Gallimard, 1958.

Memoirs of a Dutiful Daughter. Cleveland: World Publishing, 1959.

La Force de l'age (1929–1944). Paris: Gallimard, 1960.

The Prime of Life. Cleveland: World Publishing, 1962.

La Force des choses (1944–1962). Paris: Gallimard, 1963.

Force of Circumstance. New York: Putnam, 1965.

Tout compte fait (1962–1972). Paris: Gallimard, 1972.

All Said and Done. New York: Putnam, 1972.

Narrative

Une mort tres douce. Paris: Gallimard, 1964.

A Very Easy Death. New York: Putnam, 1966.

Books About Simone De Beauvoir (In English)

Ascher, Carole, *Simone de Beauvoir: A Life of Freedom*. Boston: Beacon Press, 1981.

Bieber, Konrad, *Simone de Beauvoir*. Boston: Twayne, 1975.

Cottrell, Robert D., *Simone de Beauvoir*. New York: Ungar, 1975.

Francis, Claude, and Fernande Gontier, *Simone de Beauvoir: a life ...*, New York: St. Martin's Press, 1987.

Keefe, Terri, *Simone de Beauvoir: A Study of Her Writings*. Totowa, New Jersey: Barnes & Noble, 1983.

Leighton, Jean, *Simone de Beauvoir on Women*. New Jersey: Associated University Presses, 1975.

Madsen, Axel, *Hearts and Minds*. New York: Morrow, 1977.

Marks, Elaine, *Simone de Beauvoir: Encounters with Death*. Rutgers University Press, 1973.

Schwarzer, Alice, *After The Second Sex: Conversations with Simone de Beauvoir*. Translated by Marianne Howarth. New York: Pantheon Books, 1984.

Whitmarsh, Anne, *Simone de Beauvoir and the Limits of Commitment*. London: Cambridge University Press, 1981.

Books Devoted In Part To Simone De Beauvoir

Barnes, H. E., *The Literature of Possibility*. University of Nebraska Press, 1959.

Brophy, Brigid, "Simone de Beauvoir." *Don't Never Forget: Collected Views and Reviews*. Holt, Rinehart and Winston, Inc., 1966.

Peyre, Henri, *French Novelists of Today*. New York: Oxford University Press, 1967.

Reck, R. D., *Literature and Responsibility*. Louisiana State University Press, 1969.

Periodicals

"An SR Panel Takes Aim at *The Second Sex*." (Reviewed by K. A. Menninger; Philip Wylie; Ashley Montagu; Phyllis McGinley; Margaret Mead; O. R. Goldman) *The Saturday Review*, February 21, 1953.

Dijkstra, Sandra, "Simone de Beauvoir and Betty Friedan: The Politics of Omission." *Feminist Studies* 6, No. 2 (Summer 1980).

Felstiner, Mary Lowenthal, "Seeing *The Second Sex* Through the Second Wave." *Ibid.*

Fuchs, Jo-Ann P., "Female Eroticism in *The Second Sex*." *Ibid.*

Gill, Brendan, "No More Eve." *The New Yorker*, February 28, 1953.

Hardwick, Elizabeth, *Partisan Review*, No. 3, May-June 1953.

Kluckhohn, Clyde, "The Female of Our Species." *The New York Times*, February 22, 1953.

Le Doeuff, Michele, "Simone de Beauvoir and Existentialism." *Feminist Studies* 6, No. 2 (Summer 1980).

Montagu, Ashley, "A French Gauntlet Tossed to Dr. Kinsey." *New York Herald Tribune Book Review*, February 22, 1953.

Mullahy, Patrick, "Woman's Place." *The Nation*, February 21, 1953.

Radford, C. B., "Simone de Beauvoir: Feminism's Friend or Foe?" *Nottingham French Studies*, October 1967 and May 1968.

Simon, Margaret A. and Jessica Benjamin, "Simone de Beauvoir: An Interview." *Feminist Studies* 5, No. 2 (Summer 1979).

www.ingramcontent.com/pod-product-compliance
Lightning Source LLC
LaVergne TN
LVHW011719060526
838200LV00051B/2954